Praise for

Is the Bible Good for Women?

"Is the Bible good for women? Some hear the question and scoff: 'Of course not! It's antiquated, dangerous, misogynistic.' Some hear the question and grieve: 'Of course it is! It's God's Word, and it frees women to be who God means for them to be.' What Wendy Alsup understands and articulates is that even something as good as the Bible can be put to poor use in the hands of sinful people. Thus she approaches the question with care and insight to provide an answer that is thoroughly biblical and so very satisfying."

—TIM CHALLIES, blogger and author of *Visual Theology*

"The Bible *is* good for women. Yet many misunderstandings and misapplications of the Bible's teachings harm women and, in harming women, harm the world. Providing helpful textual and contextual insights and backed by careful research and clear writing, this book shows how the Bible has always advanced the flourishing of women and can continue to do so today, if only we will read, understand, and apply it."

—KAREN SWALLOW PRIOR, author of *Booked: Literature in the Soul of Me* and *Fierce Convictions—The Extraordinary Life of Hannah More: Poet, Reformer Abolitionist*

"Wendy Alsup offers a Jesus-centered way of interpreting some difficult passages of the Bible related to women. These are passages the Bible's critics love to offer as proof that God's Word hurts women. Rather than a line-for-line rebuttal, Alsup attempts to shift the debate by providing counsel in how to read the Bible as a whole story focused on our glorious Savior. Even if you don't agree with her at every point, you'll be helped to understand the Bible better and why it's not only good but the best book for women."

—THABITI ANYABWILE, pastor of Anacostia River Church and author of *Reviving the Black Church*

"Is the Bible good for women? Many people (both women and men) would emphatically say no. To them, the Bible promotes a patriarchy that has historically crushed women and given men license to suppress and abuse them. After all, how could a book that talks about forcing a raped woman to marry her rapist or tells wives to 'submit' to their husbands be good for women? Without flinching at the difficulty of certain parts of the Bible, and while at the same time upholding divine inspiration of the Scripture, Wendy Alsup weaves together answers that are not only consistently Christ-centered but are also true to the heart of the Lord who loves women. As a woman who highly values both women and God's Word, Alsup gives us answers to some of the most difficult questions about gender in the Bible. Because her answers are deeply compassionate and true to Scripture, this book will be good for you. I highly recommend it!"

—ELYSE M. FITZPATRICK, author of *Home: How Heaven and the New Earth Satisfy Our Deepest Longings*

"Unlike other volumes with the words *women* and *Bible* in the title, *Is the Bible Good for Women?* offers readers more than lessons on femininity via the sacred text. Instead, Wendy Alsup aims to give us a better understanding of the Scripture itself, reminding men and women alike that our ultimate good is found in knowing and reflecting Christ. Whether you are on a personal journey or teaching through a difficult passage, this book provides the necessary context and story arc to understand that, yes, even in its more difficult points, the Bible truly is good news for all of us."

—HANNAH ANDERSON, speaker and author of *Made for More: An Invitation to Live in God's Image* and *Humble Roots: How Humility Grounds and Nourishes Your Soul*

"Wendy has done a magnificent job here in answering the question of the book title. If we desire women to flourish in God's good design, then we must understand from the whole of Scripture what that design is. Although I don't agree with all her conclusions, this is an excellent book that is serious about the Bible and serious about women thriving."

—MATT CHANDLER, lead pastor of the Village Church and president of Acts 29 church-planting network

"I know the Scripture is inerrant, yet the first few times I read through the whole Bible, there were directions about women that made me cringe, and I wrote in my margin, 'Help me understand, O Lord!' If you have felt like this, you will be so enlightened by *Is the Bible Good for Women?* A biblical scholar, Wendy Alsup puts these passages in the context of all of Scripture and brings light that will affirm that yes, indeed, not only is Jesus for women, but the Bible is for women! We need this not just in speaking to our secular friends but to our own souls."

—DEE BRESTIN, author of *The Friendships of Women* and *Idol Lies*

"Wendy asks penetrating questions about the Bible that have lingered in the minds of many people: Can women trust the Bible? What do we do with women like Tamar, Dinah, or the daughter of Jephthah? What about the imperatives for women to submit to husbands and church officers? Is the Bible merely a patriarchal document that supports the oppression of women, or is it God's good Word to all people? Wendy tackles these questions head on, revealing that these are not arbitrary stories and commands but rather meaningful texts that point to a reason and a hope to keep the memories of even these women alive. God does value and care for women, and we see that when we read Scripture interpreted through Christ our Lord."

—AIMEE BYRD, author of *Housewife Theologian, Theological Fitness,* and *No Little Women*

"Some pastors and laypeople treat difficult texts of Scripture like the scariest parts of a movie—taking furtive glances through barely parted fingers, fast-forwarding to the parts of the story that seem easier and happier. Others use these texts as proof points to shore up a particular framework or ideological agenda, or to tear one (or all of them) down. This book does neither. Instead, Wendy Alsup shows how reading the Bible as the cohesive story of Jesus and His work on our behalf is the answer to questions some of the most challenging texts in the Bible raise for women to read and receive as good. Whether you're a pastor or a layperson, a complementarian or an egalitarian, or whether you're someone for whom such terms create more questions than they answer, you will find insights that challenge and encourage you and be driven to deeper study and trust in the sufficiency of Scripture to answer even the hardest questions."

—RACHAEL STARKE, writer at GospelCenteredWoman.com and TheThinkingsofThings.com

IS THE

BIBLE

GOOD FOR

WOMEN?

IS THE
BIBLE
GOOD FOR
WOMEN?

Seeking Clarity and Confidence
Through a Jesus-Centered
Understanding of Scripture

MULTNOMAH

Is the Bible Good for Women?

Grateful acknowledgment is given for some content in chapter 2 that was adapted from a talk by pastor John Haralson of Grace Church Seattle and for some content in chapter 9 that was developed from a talk by professor Hans Bayer of Covenant Theological Seminary. Used by permission.

Trade Paperback ISBN 978-1-60142-900-1
eBook ISBN 978-1-60142-901-8

Copyright © 2017 by Wendy Alsup

Cover design and photography by Kristopher K. Orr

Published in the United States by Multnomah, an imprint of the Crown Publishing Group, a division of Penguin Random House LLC, New York.

MULTNOMAH® and its mountain colophon are registered trademarks of Penguin Random House LLC.

Library of Congress Cataloging-in-Publication Data
Names: Alsup, Wendy Horger, 1970– author.
Title: Is the Bible good for women? : seeking clarity and confidence through a Jesus-centered understanding of scripture / Wendy Alsup.
Description: First Edition. | Colorado Springs, Colorado : Multnomah, 2017. | Includes bibliographical references.
Identifiers: LCCN 2016039926 (print) | LCCN 2017003254 (ebook) | ISBN 9781601429001 (pbk.) | ISBN 9781601429018 (electronic)
Subjects: LCSH: Bible—Feminist criticism. | Bible and feminism. | Bible—Criticism, interpretation, etc. | Jesus Christ—Person and offices—Biblical teaching.
Classification: LCC BS521.4 .A47 2017 (print) | LCC BS521.4 (ebook) | DDC 220.6082—dc23
LC record available at https://lccn.loc.gov/2016039926

Printed in the United States of America
2017—First Edition

10 9 8 7 6 5 4 3 2 1

Special thanks to my pastors John Barnett, John Haralson, Sean Sawyers, and John Mark Patrick for the ways they have faithfully discipled me over the years in the connected, coherent story of Jesus through Scripture.

Contents

Introduction

s the Bible good for women? Growing up in the conservative South, I never considered that question. I didn't understand anything of women's rights except the caricatures I saw on the news during attempts to pass the Equal Rights Amendment. But I was one of three daughters, no sons, born to a Christian dad who valued his girls well. Though I experienced my fair share of struggles growing up, female oppression in a patriarchal society did not seem to be one of them. As I got older and watched the news with a more critical eye, a different view of women came into my line of sight. There were countries where women couldn't vote? There were cultures that would put victims of rape to death in honor killings?

Then I moved to Seattle, where women's rights and feminist issues are often center stage in local news and conversation. I couldn't hide from these issues anymore. Female mutilation, legal oppression, and culturally accepted rape were much bigger issues affecting many more women worldwide than I had ever understood. And domestic abuse, the blaming of sexual abuse survivors, and discrimination in the workforce occurred closer to home. My experience of being valued as a female by the men in my life was not the norm worldwide, but I also came to realize it wasn't the norm in the conservative South either. I was bombarded by women's issues. As a believer in Jesus since childhood and one who loved and valued the Bible, I was barraged with criticism of the Scripture around women's issues as well. Does the Bible address oppression of women in helpful ways? Or does it only perpetuate such oppression among its followers? In a world that is quite often very bad for women, does the Bible help or does it make it worse?

HARMFUL WORLDWIDE PRACTICES

National Public Radio recently highlighted a disturbing practice in western Nepal in which young women are banished to outdoor sheds when they are on their periods.[1] The families interviewed believe that the girls could cause illnesses among the family's elderly if they touch them while menstruating. The humiliation and stigma those girls endure is worth public outcry.

Hinduism is the primary religion (81 percent) in Nepal.[2] Although Judaism and Christianity have made small inroads into the country, this practice of barring young menstruating women from their homes does not seem to have a direct relationship to Old Testament Law. Yet I can't help but think of similar instructions in the Law (see Leviticus 15:19–33) when I hear of the Nepali practice. I know from Scripture that despite the similarities, the Nepali practice is a perversion of God's intent in the Law. The Nepali tradition attributes to girls on their periods something Old Testament Law never does, it does so without the Law's corresponding instruction to men, and it perpetuates a practice that

Jesus said two thousand years ago was brought to completion through Him. (We will work this out in greater detail in chapters 6 and 7.)

But the comparison puts a question to us, one that many women ask themselves: Is the Bible good for women? How can a book that includes instructions on where a woman can sleep or sit when menstruating be trusted by women today when similar modern practices like that of the Nepalese are clearly harmful for women?

We have not always been suspicious about the Bible's take on women's issues. For long periods in history, people viewed the Bible and Christianity as powers that lifted the downtrodden and demoralized to new places of respect. During the twentieth century, the first wave of feminism gave voice to women whom society had long marginalized. In 1920, women finally won the right to vote in the United States, due in large part to the efforts of Christians. The Woman's Christian Temperance Union led this movement, seeking to apply biblical principles of social justice to larger society.[3] Based in part on their understanding of Jesus and the Bible, men and women of faith fought together for women to have the right to vote. This first wave of feminism resulted in women's right to vote and inherit land, along with subsequent benefits to both women and children as women gained a voice in legislation.

But as the century wore on, there came a fork in the road in which orthodox Christianity seemed to go in one direction concerning the rights of women, and second-wave feminism (which focused on birth control, abortion rights, and equal pay) in another. In the last few years, many pro-women authors (for lack of a better name), even Christian ones, have painted a picture of women in the Bible that is troubling, even referring to certain passages concerning women in the Bible as "texts of terror."[4] According to many books and popular blogs, the view in our current culture is that an orthodox understanding of the Bible is threatening and even downright harmful to women. The similarities between Old Testament Law having to do with women on their periods and the Nepali practice that results in shaming menstruating girls seem to only reinforce such a distrust of Scripture.

Other books have dissected the history of evangelical Christianity and the secular women's movement.[5] Rather than looking at how we arrived at the twenty-first-century general mistrust of the Bible regarding women, I would like instead to simply challenge it by encouraging us to discover and use a Jesus-centered understanding of Scripture when reading the Bible. In turn, this gives us a Jesus-centered understanding of how the Bible speaks about women and to women in its pages. I believe this process will give us all a life-giving perspective of our gendered selves in God's kingdom. It will help us see the profound difference in the shame that fathers project onto menstruating Nepali daughters and the dignity God places on His.

CHECK YOUR BAGGAGE FIRST

Before we develop a Jesus-centered understanding of Scripture, let's examine any personal baggage we might bring to this study. What presuppositions and suspicions do you carry into a discussion of gender in the Bible? What can we agree on as a basic foundation to start the discussion? Secular or Christian, feminist or conservative, most everyone agrees that men and women are not exactly the same. The biological differences are obvious; the role culture takes in influencing other differences is debated. One thing is clear: the basic biological differences in XX and XY chromosomes play out both physically and mentally at some level in differences between the genders for 99 percent of humanity.*

Male and female are overlapping but distinct identifiers. Men and women have similarities as well as differences. In a Venn diagram comparing the two genders, an overlapping middle part exists between male and female. But here is where our baggage comes into play. The conversation around gender in the church often seems to involve two camps: one that loves the overlapping part of the Venn diagram of gender but feels threatened by any reference to distinctions, and one that loves the distinctions but has a narrow view of the overlap.

---

* According to the Intersex Society of North America, www.isna.org/faq/frequency, some form of biological disorder concerning gender affects approximately 1 percent of the human population. Although biological abnormalities are real, we are focusing here on the predominant statistical norms of gender.

How do you feel about the disparate nature of gender? Do you prefer to focus on the overlapping parts? Do you feel threatened by those who emphasize the distinctions? Or perhaps you find the distinctions more comfortable and feel discomfort with those who emphasize the overlap. It is helpful to acknowledge your preconceptions as you start this study.

Personally, I see a big fat middle part of overlap in my mental Venn diagram of gender as presented in Scripture. Men and women share much responsibility and authority in God's kingdom. But I also love and value the distinct elements of manhood and womanhood. I see value in both sides of the debate, and I have baggage from both sides. We have much to work through here—both you as the book's reader and I as its author!

CHECK YOUR MOTIVE

Once you have checked your baggage, it is also helpful to acknowledge your motive for reading this book. Maybe, for instance, you believe in Jesus and are curious to understand what the Bible says on women's issues. Because you love Jesus, you want to understand better the Scriptures that speak of Him. Or maybe you don't believe in Jesus and want to explore more about the Bible as you decide about Him. How can He be good in general if He is not good for women, right?

There is a third type of reader as well. You might generally believe in Jesus but are not sure what you believe about the Bible. Gandhi famously said that he liked what he knew of Christ but not what he knew of Christians. In this book, I will deal with a similar but different issue. What happens when people like what they know of Christ *but not what they know of the Bible,* particularly when it comes to women's issues? This certainly presents a problem for someone wanting to know more about Christ. How can we know Jesus in truth without confidence in the primary historical document that speaks of Him?

Despite having come to Christ at a young age, I deeply wrestled with the goodness and trustworthiness of the Bible. I knew that factual evidence existed for some of its supernatural claims. For instance, as a math teacher who appreciates science, I was intrigued that Isaiah spoke of God sitting enthroned "above the circle of the earth" (Isaiah 40:22) some two thousand years before Christopher Columbus first theorized that the earth was round. I found it noteworthy that the Old Testament lawgiver exhibited an understanding of how infectious diseases are transmitted (by sharing dirty items and touching without washing; see Leviticus 15), one that the medical community didn't discover or accept until the late 1800s. There is evidence throughout Scripture of an intelligent being with knowledge above and over mankind's directing the writing of Scripture. Yet I still could not logically argue my way into belief in the trustworthiness of Scripture. In the end I still had to take a step of faith that the Bible is what it says it is.

What exactly does the Bible claim for itself? Its claims are frankly audacious:

- Its instructions are a lamp to guide our feet along a rocky path (see Psalm 119:105).
- No author wrote on his own, but each was moved along by the Holy Spirit (see 2 Peter 1:20–21).

- All Scripture is inspired, or "breathed out," by God
  (2 Timothy 3:16–17).

Yet big issues can cause our confidence in Scripture's claims about itself to break down.

THE CHALLENGE

The first issue that can break our confidence in Scripture is that the Bible is big and complicated. It includes prophecies, laws, and history. Large sections teach how to worship God, and other sections give wise advice for living. Scripture details the development of humanity from creation until the very last days that we will live on earth as we know it. The Bible tells a long, winding story that crisscrosses itself again and again. It repeats themes through multiple books, treats the same theme from multiple angles, and teaches truths both systematically and allegorically. Many view it like a calculus textbook from which they quickly turn away because they believe that it is impossible to understand. Both new and seasoned Christians face the temptation to give up trying to understand Scripture or reconcile problem passages.

The second issue is this: if we encounter some subset of Bible truth about women, particularly troubling passages in the Law, without understanding the larger narrative of Scripture, what conclusion could we reach except that the Bible is as bad for women as the Nepali tradition is for Nepali daughters? Passages such as the Law's command to a rapist to marry his victim (see

Deuteronomy 22:28–29) or the decree to stone a woman who is not a virgin at marriage (see verses 20–21) can, at face value, seem irreconcilable with a good God. In our calculus book example, this is the same as flipping only to a complicated problem in the middle of the book without understanding how the previous chapters set up the problem or how the following chapters resolve it. We slam the book shut, believing calculus to be impractical and worthless, maybe even harmful.

Understanding the Bible does not have to be this way. The Bible does not give us problems that it does not also teach us how to solve. We have help to understand it. Who is this help? The psalmist prayed that God Himself would aid him in understanding Scripture: "Open my eyes, that I may behold wondrous things out of your law" (Psalm 119:18). His prayer reveals that although we understand God through Scripture, we also understand Scripture through God. If we believe the psalmist, there is something wonderful to be seen when we stay engaged in the struggle to understand.

If you are not confident in either Jesus or the Bible, it may feel unsettling to engage God in prayer to understand Scripture. Nevertheless, doing so is helpful at the start of this study: *God, open our eyes to see wonderful things in and through the Bible, even for those of us who are not yet sure what we believe about You or Your Scripture.*

If you come to this study questioning the goodness and trustworthiness of the Bible, I encourage you to stay engaged in the struggle.

GOD THE AUTHOR

As we begin this journey to understand the Bible and women, we should think for a moment about the One who claims to be its Author. You might not be ready to accept that there is a God and He is the author of the Bible, but it is intriguing to consider the implications if there is and if He is. For those who believe the Genesis story of creation, the God who created the world and hung the stars in the sky is a logical mathematician. He was the first Physicist and is still the ultimate Engineer. Yet this same God colored His ordered world with beautiful hues. The God revealed in the Bible is the greatest Artist and the most poetic Author. He is both left-brained and right-brained, and His written Word to us reflects both aspects of His character. The Bible is both logical and artistic. It lays a logical framework, but it fleshes out that framework with metaphor and allusion.

God primarily tells us a *story* through the Bible, one in which womanhood is a major theme and driving force in the narrative. It's been said that the Bible begins with a divorce (God's separation from His people after the fall of man) and ends with a marriage (the marriage supper of the Lamb in Revelation), and everything in between is the story of God wooing back His bride. This is a helpful way of understanding God's story to us. But it's important to remember that God actually began His story with a perfect relationship between Himself and His people, which sets the stage for the rest of the story. (I will walk through the aspects of His story to us in more detail in chapter 1.)

As we unwrap Scripture in an effort to understand whether

the Bible is good for women, I will rely greatly on a simple principle: *The Bible is the best commentary on itself.* The best way to gain clarity about others' confusing statements is to ask them exactly what they mean or to cross-reference their words with other things they've said. I love to study what others have written concerning the Bible and have learned much doing so. But we won't be able to discern whether the Bible is good for women by reading outside authors the way we can by examining what the Bible says about itself. When we connect the dots in Scripture from, say, Dinah's rape in Genesis 34 to Jesus's interaction with the woman thrown before Him to be stoned in John 8, we see an arc of story that gives meaning to a chapter in Genesis that, without New Testament commentary, ends with hopeless oppression. No outside commentary offers as much insight on Scripture as the Bible offers about itself. Various verses on the same subject serve as data points we can connect to clarify each. As we learn to use Scripture to understand Scripture, we will see that we can trust both the Bible's hard instructions to us as well as its easy encouragements, as each gives insight on the other.

Augustine said, "Whoever, then, thinks that he understands the Holy Scriptures, or any part of them, but puts such an interpretation upon them as does not . . . build up . . . this . . . love of God and our neighbor, does not yet understand them as he ought."[6] In light of Jesus's greatest command in Matthew 22 to love God and neighbor, I am burdened by the sloppy ways many popular voices, conservative and liberal, have handled Scripture at times, using it as a bludgeon on one side and discarding it as archaic and oppressive on the other. The Bible is life-giving in its instructions to men and women. When we accurately handle the Bible, it blesses us all and causes us to grow in our love for God and for others. This conviction prompted me to write the book you hold in your hands.

We will weave a tapestry in this study, focusing particularly on womanhood in some chapters and zooming out in others to the larger story of Scripture. My hope is that the garment we weave will grab you with its beauty and encourage you to stay engaged with God through His written Word. I pray we all come to a deeper understanding of the dignity God places on His daughters as they live out His good plan.

How Did Jesus Approach the Bible?

Before we investigate whether the Bible is good for women, we need to first know if the Bible is good in general. To answer that question, we need to understand Scripture. Just as calculus seems much more helpful and good to those who understand it and use it in their fields, few of us are going to value the Bible in our lives if we find it only confusing or impractical. As a math teacher, I love the moment the light comes on in the eyes of students who have struggled to understand a math concept. They move from apathy because the concept seems irrelevant to their lives or from frustration because they need to understand something they can't figure out, to perseverance and enthusiasm once they realize both that they can understand it and that it is relevant to their studies. My hope is for the light to come on similarly for you as you seek to better understand the Bible in the general sense. If you don't understand the Bible generally, you won't understand it specifically about women. In this chapter we start with Jesus

Himself, whose words about the Bible become a great tool for understanding it.

Why does the average Christian need to understand the Bible? Isn't that the job of pastors or seminary professors? Well, it is their job, but it is our job too. Lacking an understanding of Scripture is a great barrier to trusting it. Carolyn Custis James wisely said, "We ask too much of ourselves to try to trust a stranger."[1] We cannot trust a God we don't know. And we cannot know Him without understanding Him through His revelation of Himself to us through His Word. We need to know and understand Scripture to trust it and the God it tells us of, and key to such understanding is seeing how it speaks of Jesus throughout its pages. This applies, too, to those who are not yet sure what they believe about either Jesus or the Bible.

Though I know not all will agree with me, my presupposition is that God inspired Scripture and has preserved it until all He said has been proved true and witnessed by humankind. Even if you disagree with me on that point, we can at least agree that Jesus affirms this understanding of the Law in particular in the Gospels: "Truly, I say to you, until heaven and earth pass away, not an iota, not a dot, will pass from the Law until all is accomplished" (Matthew 5:18).

Whether or not you personally accept that view, come with me on a journey through the Word. I hope our time opens your eyes to the beauty of Scripture's connected story of God's love and redemption despite our sin. As Paul told his protégé Timothy, God breathed out Scripture that is "useful for teaching, rebuking, correcting and training in righteousness, so that the man [and woman] of God may be thoroughly equipped for every good work" (2 Timothy 3:16–17, NIV). May any growth we experience in understanding the Bible be followed by trust in its usefulness to us, its goodness, as we navigate life.

THE ROAD TO EMMAUS

Let's begin examining the Bible in what might seem an odd place, Luke 24. The setting is the road to Emmaus outside Jerusalem, after Jesus's resurrection but before He revealed Himself to His disciples. Two disciples were walking along the road discussing all that had happened: Jesus's ministry, His miracles, their former confidence that He was the one predicted by the prophets to free Israel from oppression, and His crucifixion, which shook everything they thought they understood about Him. As the two talked, Jesus drew near and began walking with them. They did not recognize Him even when He asked what they were talking about. After they explained what had happened the last few days, Jesus responded, "'O foolish ones, and slow of heart to believe all that the prophets have spoken! Was it not necessary that the Christ should suffer these things and enter into his glory?' And beginning with Moses and all the Prophets, he interpreted to them in all the Scriptures the things concerning himself" (verses 25–27).

Later Jesus told them,

> "These are my words that I spoke to you while I was still with you, that everything written about me in the Law of Moses and the Prophets and the Psalms must be fulfilled."

Then he opened their minds to understand the Scriptures,
and said to them, "Thus it is written, that the Christ
should suffer and on the third day rise from the dead,
and that repentance and forgiveness of sins should be
proclaimed in his name to all nations, beginning from
Jerusalem." (verses 44–47)

In this moment, Jesus decoded large portions of the Old Testament for His followers. He told His disciples how He understood Scripture and how they should too. Note that the climax of
whatever specific things Jesus told them about the Old Testament
was that Christ should suffer and rise again and that "repentance
and forgiveness of sins should be proclaimed in his name" in all
places. This is the culminating message of the Old Testament. It
is the gospel.

In Luke 24, Jesus gave us the foundation for a Jesus-centered
understanding of Scripture.

SEPARATE FILE FOLDERS OF STORIES

Unfortunately, many well-meaning Christians today use what I
refer to as a separate-file-folder approach to the stories of Scripture. In that paradigm, Psalms contains separate file folders of re-
assuring words for hard moments. The Genesis file folder is full of
interesting moral lessons. The Proverbs file is useful when one
needs good advice. The Law and Minor Prophets? Many aren't
sure of their purpose, and the file folders containing those Old
Testament stories often gather dust. In the very back of the file

cabinet, with a "Do Not Touch" note on them, are the files containing troubling stories, such as Dinah's abuse in Genesis 34, archaic instructions of Deuteronomy 22 for those who are raped, and the rape and dismemberment of the concubine in Judges 19.

This separate-file-folder approach to the Bible misses the connections between the Old Testament and the good news that Jesus explained on the road to Emmaus. The solution is for us to follow the references to Jesus and His coming sacrifice through the Old Testament. Once we understand how to look for connections to the gospel in the Old Testament, the separate file folders open up. The characters stumble out of our filing cabinet, joining hands story by story from the first of Genesis until Jesus appears in person in Matthew. Each story feeds into the larger story of God's good plan before time began to redeem His people.

What story did Jesus weave for His disciples on the road to Emmaus? I wish I could have heard Him in person, because I imagine His instructions were much better than my attempt. But I believe He hit on the themes that follow in this chapter, the pictures of Him throughout the Old Testament that had many watchful for Him when He arrived in person in the New Testament. As Philip announced to Nathanael, "We have found him of whom Moses in the Law and also the prophets wrote, Jesus of Nazareth, the son of Joseph" (John 1:45).

THE SCARLET THREAD

The phrase "scarlet thread," first popularized in a sermon by W. A. Criswell, comes from Israelite spies' interactions with the prostitute

Rahab in Joshua 2:18 (NASB). The spies instructed Rahab to put a scarlet cord, or thread, in her window so the Israelites wouldn't attack her and her family during the destruction of Jericho. Did the color of the cord reflect the blood of Jesus? The Bible does not say exactly, but the general situation reminds us of God's wrath sparing the Israelites in Egypt who had the mark of blood on their doorposts at the first Passover, which was certainly a reference to Jesus's shedding of blood on the cross. When pastors or teachers refer to the scarlet thread in the Bible, the color scarlet reflects the color of Jesus's blood, and the concept of thread reflects the way the blood weaves itself through the stories of the Old Testament to form the fabric of understanding of what that blood would accomplish for us in the New.

As we walk through this theme of Scripture, it is easy to get bogged down in the details. It may help to think of this chapter as a prerequisite class for a course of study that inspires you. The prerequisites can feel like a burden that you want to get through quickly to get to the good stuff. But a good prerequisite class gives foundational material you will need later. That is what this chapter does, and I hope you will persevere, because what you learn here will form the basis on which we build the rest of the book. (I promise, we'll get back to women and the Bible shortly!)

THE SCARLET THREAD WITH ADAM AND EVE

To understand the story of Jesus in the Old Testament, we must remember that God is both Engineer and Artist, left-brained and right-brained, and His Word reflects both aspects of His character. He opened the Bible in the classic form of the best of authors. All was well and beautiful in God's perfect, new creation. But evil quickly entered the scene as the enemy of all enemies dealt a devastating blow against mankind. Yet, in the midst of the fallout of Adam and Eve's sin, God gave the first premonition of coming rescue: "I will put enmity between you and the woman, and between your offspring and her offspring; he shall bruise your head, and you shall bruise his heel" (Genesis 3:15).

And so the good news of Jesus begins in Genesis. This is the first hint of the coming Messiah. In essence God said to Satan, "You will have enmity [or warfare] with One born of woman. He will permanently damage you, while you will only wound Him." This is also the first hint of God's good news, particularly for women. Despite woman's role in the Fall, she would be the one to bear the Savior into the world.

God then killed an animal for the first time and used the skins to cover Adam and Eve's nakedness. In the death of that first animal, the scarlet thread began, the poetic trickle of blood running throughout the Old Testament that points to Jesus's coming death on the cross.

THE SCARLET THREAD
THROUGH CAIN AND ABEL

After God killed an animal to cover Adam and Eve's nakedness, blood next poured out in Genesis 4 as their son Cain killed his brother Abel in a jealous rage. The story of Abel's death may initially seem unimportant, perhaps just a moral lesson on acceptable sacrifices to God, as I was taught as a kid in Sunday school. But later we learn that Abel's blood teaches us something about God's plan to save His children. Abel joins hands in the long line of characters in Scripture ultimately pointing to Jesus: "By faith Abel offered to God a more acceptable sacrifice than Cain, through which he was commended as righteous, God commending him by accepting his gifts. And through his faith, though he died, he still speaks" (Hebrews 11:4).

Abel died walking forward in his faith, obedient to God. His blood was shed in faith, and his story is in the Bible to communicate something to us about faith, blood, and death. Yet Hebrews also teaches that Abel's story is an imperfect allusion to Jesus's better sacrifice. Hebrews 12:24 refers "to Jesus, the mediator of a new covenant, and to the sprinkled blood that speaks a better word than the blood of Abel." Whatever Abel's sacrifice communicated, Jesus's communicates something much, much better.

When we let the Bible explain the Bible, we learn from Hebrews that those first moments of humanity were already giving us hints about what Jesus would come to do once and for all on the cross, the righteous dying while the unrighteous receive mercy.

THE SCARLET THREAD THROUGH ABRAHAM

After giving us small glimpses in the opening chapters of Genesis of His big plan for redemption, God moved the narrative to an entirely different level with the story of Abraham. Abraham wasn't an allusion to what God was going to do. Abraham was where God actually started doing it! The account of Abraham appears in

Genesis 11–25. Hear how the apostle Paul described Abraham's story in Galatians 3:6–8: "'He believed God, and it was credited to him as righteousness.' Understand, then, that those who believe are children of Abraham. The Scripture foresaw that God would justify the Gentiles by faith, and announced the gospel in advance to Abraham: 'All nations will be blessed through you'" (NIV).

When did God first announce the gospel to Abraham? Paul was referring to a long interaction between God and Abraham in Genesis 12–17. We often think of the gospel as a succinct summary of Christ's death in our place. But Paul used the word to refer holistically to the long story of Jesus in Scripture, in this case the promises in Genesis that one would come through Abraham's lineage to bless all people.

> The LORD said to Abram, "... I will make of you a great nation, and I will bless you and make your name great, so that you will be a blessing.... And in you all the families of the earth shall be blessed." (12:1–3)

> He brought [Abraham] outside and said, "Look toward heaven, and number the stars, if you are able to number them." Then he said to him, "So shall your offspring be." And he believed the LORD, and he counted it to him as righteousness. (15:5–6)

God then promised to give Abraham possession of the land he occupied and made a covenant with him, commanding him to bring a heifer, goat, ram, dove, and pigeon to sacrifice. Abraham cut and arranged the dead animals, then fell into a deep sleep: "When the sun had gone down and it was dark, behold, a smoking fire pot and a flaming torch passed between these pieces. On that day the LORD made a covenant with Abram, saying, 'To your offspring I give this land, from the river of Egypt to the great river, the river Euphrates'" (15:17–18).

Again, we see the scarlet thread in this bloody covenant of Genesis 15, one that feels foreign to many twenty-first-century believers. But such a blood covenant was familiar to the people at the time as a symbolic contract between two parties to seal a relationship. Note the unique thing about this particular covenant: though God tasked Abraham with assembling the parts of the ceremony, the ceremony itself had only one active participant, God Himself. Abraham was asleep the entire time God was sealing this covenant with him. A smoking fire pot and blazing torch passed between the divided parts of the bloody sacrifice, both symbolic pictures indicating God's presence, not Abraham's.

It helps us to understand the symbolism of this ceremony by jumping to the story of Hosea and Gomer much later in the Old Testament. There, by taking both parts of the covenant, we start to fully realize just what God was communicating in Genesis 15. God instructed Hosea, as a picture of God's love for His people, to take a bride who ran from him and ended up in slavery. Hosea redeemed her from slavery despite her betrayal of him, restoring her as his wife. Gomer wasn't saved from slavery because of her own good works but because of Hosea's unconditional commitment to her. Though His bride—the family of Christians—is often faithless, even running away from their commitment to their Groom, God still pursues us.

In His covenant with Abraham in Genesis 15, God first demonstrated this persevering scriptural truth. And He did it by commanding Abraham to shed blood via the sacrifice that alluded again to Jesus's coming sacrifice. God took responsibility for both sides of the covenant, and we know that it will be fulfilled, for it doesn't depend on Abraham's faithfulness but on God's. As 2 Timothy 2:13 tells us, "If we are faithless, he remains faithful—for he cannot deny himself."

At this point of Genesis, very little if any written Word of God existed. Abraham learned of God's plan through conversation. God did not dump onto Abraham a two-thousand-page treatise of systematic theology. Instead, He unfurled His plan for redemption one step at a time. As He did with Adam and Eve in Genesis 3:15, God gave just the bud of the flower of redemption in His conversations with Abraham. We know that God was doing something special through Abraham that would eventually bless all nations (see 12:3), and we know He was going to do it through Abraham's descendants (see 17:16, 19). Beyond that, at this point we are not sure what this flower would look like when it fully bloomed.

The climax of God's story didn't take clear shape until Jesus rose from the dead in the Gospels. Then, suddenly, much that was written before made sense. After Jesus's ascension to heaven, the apostles, under the inspiration of the Spirit, put the final touches on this story, and we see that the bud given in Genesis 12–17 bloomed into what we now call the gospel, or good news. As Paul wrote in Galatians 3, "The Scripture, foreseeing that God would justify the Gentiles by faith, preached the gospel beforehand to Abraham, saying, 'In you shall all the nations be blessed.' . . . And if you are Christ's, then you are Abraham's offspring, heirs according to promise" (verses 8, 29).

JOSEPH AND THE SCARLET THREAD

After God made the covenant with Abraham in Genesis 12–17, the next twenty chapters of Genesis focus on Abraham's son Isaac and Isaac's sons, Jacob and Esau. The progression of the story slows down in Genesis 37–50 to concentrate on one of Jacob's younger sons, Joseph, who was Abraham's great-grandson.

Joseph's older brothers sold him into slavery, and he ended up in Egypt. There God maneuvered circumstances so that Joseph became second-in-command of Egypt, moving him through a dream to prepare the area for a severe famine. At the height of the famine, Joseph's struggling family—including his father, his brothers, and their wives and children (who would eventually become the nation of Israel)—was close to being wiped out by starvation. Joseph's brothers traveled to Egypt desperate for food, which Joseph provided for them along with respite, safety, and forgiveness for their betrayal.

Joseph recognized the profound meaning of the moment that he was able to save his family. He said to his brothers, "As for you, you meant evil against me, but God meant it for good, to bring it about that many people should be kept alive, as they are today"

(Genesis 50:20). God sent Joseph to Egypt to prepare a way for his family, Abraham's descendants from the covenant of Genesis 12–17, to be preserved. The winding story of the tiny family of Abraham that grew to great strength and influence as the nation of Israel is full of moments like this. Although God's people were often on the verge of devastation, He again and again saved them. These were His people through whom He would eventually send the Messiah.

These stories in the Old Testament pay special attention to the line of Abraham through the firstborn sons. One clear revelation from the stories of Abraham, Isaac, Jacob, and Judah is that God didn't choose His children based on their noble character. He didn't pick the wisest, biggest, or strongest. In fact, we are hard-pressed at every turn to find qualities that recommend them. Yet God was faithful to His covenant with Abraham despite their weaknesses.

At this point, women were mostly supporting characters in the stories of these men. But if we treat Scripture as one long story, then as we continue to connect the dots, we will see both the relevance of these stories of the line of the Messiah to women and the relevance of the women in these stories to the line of the Messiah. At this point, I do want to challenge any assumption that because these stories are not dominated by female characters, they aren't important to women. Remember, in our Venn diagram of gender, there was much overlap between the genders, and subsequently there is much overlap in the relevance of stories of particular men to us as women. Most of all, despite the dominance of male characters in these stories, they are primarily stories of how

Jesus came to be born the rightful Messiah, King of the Jews.
That is highly relevant to women!

At the end of Joseph's story in Genesis 50, the children
of Israel were protected from famine in Egypt. After several
generations of growing in numbers and influence, they had become the size of a small nation. Then, instead of enjoying the
protection of the pharaoh who had set up Joseph as second-in-
command, they became slaves under a different pharaoh who
never knew Joseph.

THE SCARLET THREAD THROUGH
MOSES AND THE LAW

At this point in God's story, the allusions to Jesus rise in volume
through the account of Moses, the deliverer, as he led God's children out of slavery in Egypt. We also get new glimpses of the final
deliverance God will bring us through Jesus, particularly through
the story of the first Passover, where God saved from destruction
all those who painted the blood of a lamb on their doorpost (see
Exodus 12).

After their deliverance from Egypt, God told His people
through Moses to sacrifice animals to atone for their sins against
the laws God had given them. God gave detailed instructions
for a tent that would house the ark of the covenant, an ornate
box that held the stone tablets containing the Ten Commandments that God gave Moses at Mount Sinai after the exodus of
Israel from Egypt. This ark was placed in the Holy of Holies, an
inner room in the tabernacle that represented God's presence

among His people. Once the people received these sacrificial laws and put His practices into place at the temple, there was a clear, specific representation of what Jesus's coming sacrifice would look like (the shedding of blood of one without blemish) and what it would accomplish (atonement of sins that brings open access to God).

As we look back, the temple sacrificial system didn't seem to actually appease God. He told His people at times that He despised their sacrifices and religious festivals because their hearts were still far from Him (see Isaiah 29:13). God longed for their hearts' devotion more than their physical sacrifices of animals. Instead of what they did for God, the temple sacrifices seem most important for what they communicated to His children. Year after year, century after century, these sacrifices communicated to the Israelites—and now to us—their separation from God because of their sin and God's plan to reconcile them to Himself by placing the punishment for their sin on another.

Entwined in the tapestry of this story of blood and sacrifice is Jesus's lineage. We meet Rahab and Ruth, Boaz and Samuel. Each of their stories leads us to the emergence of King David on the scene. David's rule seems to be the high point in the history of Israel, and the later historical stories of the Old Testament wind down to Israel's becoming a marginalized nation, once great, under the rule of another. When the Gospels open in Matthew 1 with the lineage of Jesus, we finally see why these stories of who gave birth to whom are key. Just as God first promised to Abraham in Genesis, we see from His lineage that Jesus is the Son of Abraham and Son of David. We see too the importance of the

stories of women such as Tamar, Rahab, and Ruth as we understand their roles in producing Jesus the Messiah.

THE SIGNIFICANCE OF THE SCARLET THREAD

In this weaving together of the story of the Old Testament, four
simple categories help identify how each part points to Jesus in the
New Testament:

1. The easiest category is made up of passages or verses
   that offer *prophecies of the coming Messiah,* such as
   the Genesis 3:15 reference to Eve's seed defeating
   Satan. Isaiah 53 and 61 are other examples.
2. Then we find *stories that show God's work to preserve
   the lineage of Christ,* such as Joseph's actions in Egypt
   that kept Abraham's descendants from dying out.
   Esther, Rahab, and Ruth's stories fall into this
   category as well.
3. We also see *pictures of the coming Christ, His work,
   and His kingdom.* The Old Testament sacrificial
   system clearly illustrates this. The story of Hosea and
   Gomer pictures Jesus's coming redemption of His
   bride, as God instructed Hosea to pursue and restore
   Gomer despite her adultery (see Hosea 1:2–3). Boaz
   and Ruth's story reflects aspects of the gospel as well,
   as Boaz took his place as Ruth's kinsman-redeemer
   (see Ruth 2–3), foreshadowing Jesus's redemption of
   His bride, the church.

4. Many stories simply *reinforce our need for a Savior.*
Stories such as the rape and dismemberment of the
concubine of an unnamed Levite in Judges 19
reinforce the Israelites' warped sense of right and
wrong, inability to be righteous on their own, and
need for salvation through Christ.

Most parts of the Old Testament will fit one or more of these
four categories.

The scarlet thread began in Genesis with an allusion to Satan's defeat and the first animal sacrifice. It continued through
Abel's death and the blood sacrifice at the covenant between God
and Abraham. With the bloody Passover and then the institution
of the Old Testament sacrificial system, the allusions to Christ
took off. When Jesus held up the cup and proclaimed, "This is my
blood of the covenant, which is poured out for many for the forgiveness of sins" (Matthew 26:28), the scarlet thread was knotted
and secured into the garment of God's story. At this point in
Scripture, the allusions to the future shedding of blood end. With
Christ the shedding of blood was over once and for all. Yet, in
some sense, the thread continues today for those of us who practice Communion, though we use wine instead of animal blood to
reflect it. The symbols of bread representing Christ's body and
wine representing His blood remind us that even today Jesus's
blood shed for us so long ago cleanses us from our sin.

The scarlet thread of blood sacrifice and the familial thread of
the sons of Abraham through which this Savior was promised to
come are major themes throughout the Old Testament pointing

to the good news of Jesus Christ. Follow these threads and you will understand much of God's Word to us through the Old Testament.

In the book of Luke, John the Baptist's father, Zechariah, recognized the significance of both John's birth and Jesus's imminent one:

Praise be to the Lord, the God of Israel,
 because he has come and has redeemed his people.
He has raised up a horn of salvation for us
 in the house of his servant David
(as he said through his holy prophets of long
  ago). (Luke 1:68–70, NIV)

Like Zechariah, when we understand the significance of these Old Testament stories about the coming Messiah, we are able to recognize Jesus as their fulfillment. As Jesus taught His disciples in Luke 24, we then better understand both the Old Testament through Jesus and Jesus through the Old Testament. As we dig deeper together in troubling Old Testament passages, their connectedness to Jesus is key to making sense of them and discovering how God is good through them for men *and* women.

What Was Good in the Beginning?

To understand the Bible's view of women, we must start at the beginning, when "God created the heavens and the earth" (Genesis 1:1). We can't make sense of later passages concerning women in Ephesians or 1 Timothy, or even ones in Proverbs 31 or Deuteronomy, without going back to the first chapters of Genesis and understanding God's good plan at creation. God didn't write standalone books of the Bible, nor did He write standalone instructions on gender. When we isolate single passages and discuss them outside the context of Genesis 1 and 2, discussions of gender in the Bible quickly break down into stereotypes and caricatures. God wove a connected, multifaceted story, and the next thousand chapters of that story lose their meaning and purpose unless we understand the first two.

The first two chapters of the Bible focus on God's plan for all of us in perfection, and though these stories are familiar to many of us, it is valuable to look at them again to see what God planned particularly for women. These first two chapters of the Bible help us understand the vision God calls women toward throughout Scripture, even when humanity is far from Him.

PROGRESSION TOWARD PERSONHOOD

Before God describes creating woman specifically in Genesis 2, He tells us about creating mankind in general in Genesis 1. Personhood preceded womanhood. And before He describes creating mankind, He tells us about creating the earth on which mankind would live. We cannot responsibly discuss God's purposes for women without working through this progression step by step in Scripture. So look at the opening moments of the creation story in Genesis. We are setting up a foundation that we will use throughout this text, more of our prerequisites for understanding everything else.

When God created the heavens and the earth, the earth was "without form and void" (Genesis 1:2). It was confused, empty, primordial chaos. Earth couldn't support life, setting the stage for God's actions starting in verse 3. God moved into the chaos and brought order, beauty, and fullness of life. This is profound. Genesis 1 speaks first of separating the light from darkness (see verse 4) and dry land from water (see verses 6–7). It then speaks of adding vegetation, plants, and fruit trees (see verses 11–12); sun, moon, and stars (see verses 14–15); and marine life, flying fowl, and land-based animals (see verses 22–24).

Note what happens in this chapter of Genesis as we progress toward the creation of the first humans, Adam and Eve. God moved into the disarray of a creation not yet fully formed and brought forth a beautiful earth full of potential that would reflect His glory. He separated earth and sky, land and sea, and then filled each part with living plants and creatures. Finally, He crowned His creation with the act of forming mankind.

> Then God said, "Let us make man in our image, after our likeness. And let them have dominion over the fish of the sea and over the birds of the heavens and over the livestock and over all the earth and over every creeping thing that creeps on the earth."
>
> So God created man in his own image,
> > in the image of God he created him;
> > male and female he created them. (verses 26–27)

In verse 26, Scripture uses the generic word *man*, which indicates humanity as a whole. But God specifies male and female clearly in verse 27. Both genders were made to image God fully into the world.

MANKIND IN GOD'S IMAGE

What does it mean to *image* God? Despite familiarity with this story, have you ever really studied the meaning behind this first thing God says about His purpose and plan for mankind? The Hebrew word translated "image," *tselem,* means "likeness."[1] Kings in Bible times often used physical representations, or statues, in their likenesses to represent their rule in another land. For instance, Nebuchadnezzar did this in Daniel 3 with the massive statue that the captive Israelites Shadrach, Meshach, and Abednego refused to worship. When God uses this language of imagery in Genesis 1, the implication is that we represent God in the land. We are His likeness.

God completed His work in creation and told man and woman to have dominion over the earth. He made humankind His representative rulers on earth—His vicegerents, meaning persons "appointed to exercise all or some of the authority of another, especially the administrative powers of a ruler."[2]

This powerful moment in creation set the stage for everything else. It points to God's humility, which seems an odd way to think of the God who just created a glorious world out of nothing. But God, in essence, delegated His earthly rule to us. In the vernacular, God showed in this moment that He is not a control freak. It points as well to the dignity God placed on people as His image bearers. Note the beautiful, honoring commission God gave humankind in this moment.

> God blessed them. And God said to them, "Be fruitful
> and multiply and fill the earth and subdue it, and have
> dominion over the fish of the sea and over the birds of the
> heavens and over every living thing that moves on the
> earth." And God said, "Behold, I have given you every
> plant yielding seed that is on the face of all the earth, and
> every tree with seed in its fruit. You shall have them for
> food. And to every beast of the earth and to every bird of
> the heavens and to everything that creeps on the earth,

everything that has the breath of life, I have given every green plant for food." And it was so. (verses 28–30)

In this amazing moment of Scripture, God the Creator said to man and woman, "Because I made you like Me, in My image, go and do what I just did." God gave them everything He had just made to use and to steward. God tasked man and woman together to carry out these commands: to be fruitful and multiply, subdue the earth, and fill it. He wanted them to exercise agency, to move into the earth and change things. He wanted them to fill the world with life and beauty.

WOMAN IN GOD'S IMAGE

Genesis 2 then zooms in on the creation of the woman. It gives a different angle on the same story of Genesis 1. Note what was happening immediately before God created the woman: "The LORD God took the man and put him in the garden of Eden to work it and keep it. . . . Then the LORD God said, 'It is not good that the man should be alone; I will make him a helper fit for him'" (2:15, 18). God noted that it was not good for man to do this work alone and created the woman to join him. But to join him in doing what? The answer is the task of verse 15, to *work* and to *keep* the garden. The Hebrew text uses the words *abad,* which can be translated "to labor, serve, or work for another," and *shamar,* which can be translated "to keep, guard, or watch over."[3] Theologians call this passage along with Genesis 1:28–30 the creation mandate. You may recognize the vernacular of this instruction that has infiltrated the mottoes of many government institutions: to serve and protect.

The generosity of God here is staggering. He basically said to Adam and Eve, "Creation is yours." At this point there was no music, no literature, no architecture; there were no fine wines, no exquisite meals, no engineering marvels, and no scientific advances. He sent man and woman into the newly formed creation filled with plants and animals but still somewhat chaotic, and He told them to do what He'd just done: Bring order to earth. Fill it with life and new things. Subdue it. Rule it. Serve it. Protect it.

We see that man is needed. He's integral to reflecting God's glory in the world. When a man refuses to engage with his family, his work, or his community, he is living out the antithesis of God's purpose for him. We see too that woman is necessary. She is needed to reflect God's glory into the world, to walk side by side with man into the chaos to bring order, beauty, life, and fullness. In Genesis 2, God observed that it was not good for man to be alone. In the task God planned for mankind of tending and keeping, serving and protecting God's creation, one gender wasn't adequate.

Is Marriage the Goal?

Does Genesis 2 teach that marriage is the ultimate goal for every man and woman? In Eden, they say, it wasn't good that the man was alone, and God created a woman so he could be married to her. That is how it at first appears, and without further study we might argue that marriage was the supreme manifestation of the purpose of creating two genders. The implication, then, for today would be that those who never marry will have lesser earthly experiences of God's plans for their lives.

But remember, the Bible is the best commentary on itself. Our understanding of God's description of this first sinless perfection is informed by glimpses the Bible gives us of the second. In Luke 20:35, when discussing perfection in heaven, Jesus clearly states that we "neither marry nor are given in marriage" in eternity. If you cross-reference this with the marriage supper of the Lamb in Revelation 19:6–10, you could say that believers do marry but that Jesus is the only true Groom. Jesus shot down the idea that the ultimate perfection for men and women is human marriage to each other.

Understanding this also frees us from misapplying Paul's teaching on husbands and wives in Ephesians 5. Some teach that Ephesians 5 gives humankind's ultimate created purpose: men to reflect Jesus through marriage and women to reflect the church.[4] In that paradigm, marriage is the ultimate outcome for men and women, and many of God's created purposes are lost among single men and women. Christian marriage can and should be a living testimony of God's relationship with His church, but it's a metaphor, a picture. The essence of our creation is that man and woman are made in God's image and the "not good" of one gender isn't solved singularly by marriage.

Although human marriage between men and women doesn't persevere into eternity, relationship does. Relationship and community, brotherhood and sisterhood—not marriage—are the "good" of two genders from Genesis 2:18 that endures into eternity future.

We are all elbows, fingers, knees, and knuckles in the body of Christ. We need each other to function. Even in perfection, man made in the image of God needed others to accomplish the work God gave him. He couldn't serve and protect creation all by himself. And he needed another not exactly like him. He needed woman.

Certainly, marriage is a major earthly manifestation of this benefit. Marriage is good, and a husband who finds a godly wife has found a great help in serving God's purposes. But marriage is not the only manifestation of this truth. God created us, married or single, for community with both Him and others. Deeply embedded in what it means to be a human in the likeness of God is that we need relationship.

At this point in the Genesis creation account, God created a perfect world that needed tending and handed it over to His created masterpiece, man and woman. And so we see the foundational mission of God's children in perfection: "Go and do what I have done as My vicegerents on earth." And it was very good.

THE FALL AND REDEMPTION

But Genesis 1 and 2 are quickly followed by Genesis 3. The world fell into sin, and chaos reigned again. As humanity struggled through the chaos for millennia, Jesus entered into it. He was born, He lived, and He died. And then He swallowed up sin and death by rising from the dead. From there, God began His global restoration project.

Note how Jesus initiated this restoration of humanity shortly after His resurrection: He handed it back over to God's image bearers, His disciples, the church. Jesus's final words before His ascension to heaven, the Great Commission in Matthew 28:18– 20, are pivotal and profound. Jesus didn't stay on earth physically to accomplish God's plan; He, as His Father did in the Garden of Eden, sent His people into the turmoil to bring the good news of Jesus's kingdom to the world. God tasked the disciples to be His vicegerents once again. He dignified the human race anew with the Great Commission by saying, in essence, "Subdue the earth and fill it, but now the focus of such filling is the good news of God's coming kingdom through Christ."

I love the term *commission*. I know from my ninth-grade Latin class that the prefix *com-* means "with" or "together." Jesus invites His followers to join with Him in mission. Commission is different from submission, where one gets in line behind a commander leading others. Though we certainly submit to God in obedience to His kingdom commands, this Great Commission has a different emphasis. God invites us to value and live out the mission as He does. He invites us to participate in it together with Him.

The work of this "co-mission" in light of redemption is not so different from what I envision would have happened with Adam and Eve, if not for the fall of man, as they extended out from the garden. Consider the apostle Paul's discussion of creation in Romans 8:19–21: "The creation waits with eager longing for the revealing of the sons of God. For the creation was subjected to futility, not willingly, but because of him who subjected it, in hope that the creation itself will be set free from its bondage to corruption and obtain the freedom of the glory of the children of God."

This is the commission that God through Jesus again gives us: go, tell the world, spread the good news of redemption to all of creation. What nobility we see in the Great Commission when we read it in light of the creation mandate of Genesis 1. God is reclaiming what He created us to be, His vicegerents on earth, stewarding His creation in His image. How inspiring for both men and women!

Men and women have been created to sing together—to work in harmony in God's world to fulfill His plan. God created man and woman for this purpose in perfection before the Fall. And He clearly did it again after the Resurrection as He sent His disciples to reclaim the world in His name. We bear a collective responsibility to steward and bear God's image into His world. This collective responsibility is not without distinctions for each gender. We sing in harmony, where each gender's voice enhances the other, rather than in unison, which meshes the two without distinction. Yet from Genesis 1 and again in the Resurrection witness, we see that this responsibility is indeed collective. It is accomplished by two genders acting in cohort.

Carolyn Custis James wrote,

> God . . . envisioned his sons and daughters forging a
> Blessed Alliance that would become an unstoppable force
> for good in this world. We know this because when he
> created his male and female image bearers, Genesis tells

us "God blessed them" and then spread before them the global mandate to rule and subdue on his behalf. Like the owner of a cosmic family business, God deployed his sons and daughters to fulfill his good purposes throughout the earth. In a sense, the cross isn't the only vulnerable moment for God, for at creation he is vulnerable too— lavishing a world on us, giving us the place of highest honor in his heart, and setting us free to make the most of it—with every intention of looking on our efforts together like a proud Father.[5]

This inspiring image of mankind, male and female, living out God's creation mandate in this fallen world is foundational to the Bible's equally inspiring vision for women in particular. We will focus on the creation of woman specifically in the next chapter to understand this vision.

What Were We Made to Be?

I f you know what God created in perfection, you will begin to recognize it when you see it in redemption.

We want to know if the Bible is to be trusted when it speaks about women. To get to the answer, we need to understand how the Bible speaks *of* women and *to* women. We need to understand what the Bible tells us about specific women of the past and what it directs us toward today. We talked in chapter 2 about how God speaks of mankind in general in Genesis 1. Now let's focus on how God speaks of women in particular in Genesis 2.

We see two big truths for women in Genesis 1 and 2. First, when God made woman in His image, He gave her *dignity in her inherent identity*. Second, He gave her *purpose in His larger plan*. God gave woman overlapping purpose with man: the task of stewarding His creation, fruitfully multiplying, and ruling over the earth. He also gave woman *particular* purpose, wrapped up in the term *ezer,* which we will explore in depth.

Could God have made His world without women? Probably. Could He have made it without men? That is equally probable. But what loss without the two distinct but overlapping genders to reflect the fullness of the glory of God and to steward, serve, and protect His creation. God looked on His perfect creation and stated profoundly that one gender without the other was *not good* for the purposes He had planned for them.

Let's explore this vision in perfection of two distinct but overlapping genders as it pertains to women.

DIGNITY IN OUR IDENTITY

When God said in Genesis 1, "Let us make man in our image, after our likeness," He gave us the foundational purpose for mankind in general and male and female in particular. God then did exactly what He said, creating mankind in His own image, including the two genders. Before moving on, you and I must understand the profound implications for men and women of being made in God's likeness.

We must recognize who we are intended to be as women before we can understand our roles in the world. "We must find a North Star. And not simply because our circumstances change, but because we ourselves are more than the roles we play in this present world. We are large, deep, eternal beings, and only something larger and deeper and more eternal will satisfy the questions in our souls."[1]

God made us after His likeness. This makes *Him* our North Star. He is the goal. In the previous chapter we talked about God's profound vision for humankind from one angle, that of image bearers as God's vicegerents on earth, but we haven't yet exhausted the profound nature of this truth. God created woman (as well as man) to reflect and portray something about the incredible character of her Maker: His desire for relationship, His compassion, His wisdom, His strength, His knowledge, His care for the smaller and lesser, His justice, His mercy, His complexity, His creativity, His artistry.

He made woman in His tselem. In chapter 2, we saw how this word can reflect a tangible, physical representation of something. But consider now other ways this word is used in the Bible.

In the Old Testament, tselem is translated "form," "image," "likeness," or "phantom." It is derived from a Hebrew word for "shade."[2] The word seems less concrete than the other Hebrew word for idols, which were tangible representations of a god. In contrast, you could say that God created you and me to offer shades of the one true God to those watching. Ghostlike, delicate, even fleeting at times, we are fluid representations of our Creator. We are not concrete icons. We aren't hewn out of rock or molded out of gold like an idol.

We may be tall or short. Our hair and skin colors vary. But these physical things aren't the essence of tselem. Despite those differences, we mirror something real of God. Picture reflecting pools in front of a majestic mountain. The wind blows, and ripples shift the image. No two pools reflect the vision in the exact same way at any given moment, yet the cumulative effect is clear. Similarly, you and I are ethereal projections of a concrete God. Despite the individual physical differences in us, we reflect Him nonetheless.

IMAGE-BEARING HELP

After Genesis 1 gives an overview of mankind created in the image of God, reflecting Him in a unique way, Genesis 2 describes the creation of the first woman. What shades of His likeness do women particularly reflect? Genesis 2:18 provides our first key: "The LORD God said, 'It is not good for the man to be alone. I will make a helper suitable for him'" (NIV).

Much of God's vision for image-bearing womanhood is wrapped up in the single word *helper*. For many years, even as an earnest Christian girl hoping to grow up to be a faithful Christian woman, I secretly chafed at this concept. The word *help* didn't inspire me. It felt condescending. An image of a 1950s female secretary and her sexist, chain-smoking male boss came to mind.

Or worse.

I grew up in rural South Carolina, in an area that was functionally segregated despite minorities' legal gains in the 1960s. I knew what it meant to be "the help," and in my experience, it was a degrading way to refer to someone, not reflective of his inherent dignity.

Yet God says in perfection that He created woman to be a helper. It's a word we could easily misinterpret, so it's important we let the Bible explain the Bible to us. With some simple study, we see that this straightforward verse reflects something profound in terms of God's purposes for mankind in general and women in particular. The woman's part in the reflecting pool of God's character is beautiful!

Remember that Genesis 1 tells us that woman was created in

the likeness of God to steward creation with man. Genesis 2 doesn't establish a separate stream of thought for women. Instead, it intensifies what's in Genesis 1. We'll look deeper at the Hebrew word for "helper," *ezer,* but let's first reflect on the larger context: relationship with the man. From there, the nuances of ezer come into focus.

GOD, THE FIRST HELPER

Remember that Jesus's words on the second eternal perfection (the first perfection being the Garden of Eden before the Fall) from Luke 20 teach us that marriage is not the eternal answer to the "not good" of man's creation. More than marriage and procreation is needed to meet the need of men for women and women for men in the reflecting pool of the kingdom of God. Jesus was helped by Mary of Bethany and Paul by Phoebe. Lois and Eunice helped Timothy, and while Priscilla helped her husband, Aquila, she also helped Apollos. In this context of community and relationship between the genders, the brotherhood and sisterhood of the family of God, consider the Hebrew term (ezer) for this first woman, created in perfection in the image of God. She was designed and gifted particularly to be a helper suitable for Adam. There was something special about this woman that was suitable for the man.

The distinct aspects of their separate genders aided the overlapping traits. They fit each other. This certainly is visible in Christian marriage. But the fitting nature of woman to man is valuable beyond Christian marriage. Consider the male church

elders who solicit input and feedback from women in their congregation. Or the male student who listens to his female teacher.
Or the father who asks his daughter's help and the son who values
his mother's voice. The giftings of womanhood fit the needs of
manhood. In Christ, the woman gifts her male counterpart with
appropriate help. She is specifically gifted in ways he particularly
needs.

God calls this suitable, fitting thing she brings to mankind
help. It sounds like a generic term. *Help* could mean anything,
right? But each use in the Old Testament fleshes out this help so
we have a concrete vision of what God means. The Bible uses this
Hebrew word in a sober, strong way that reflects meaning deeper
than traditionally inferred in our culture. The Hebrew word
means to give succor, support and aid, to those in distress. The
word *ezer* is used twenty-one times in the Old Testament, sixteen
of which are descriptions of God Himself.[3] This frequency of use
reflects the fact that the woman was created to image the likeness
of God. Consider the use of *ezer* in Deuteronomy 33:29: "Blessed
are you, O Israel! Who is like you, a people saved by the LORD?
He is your shield and *helper* and your glorious sword. Your enemies will cower before you, and you will trample down their high
places" (NIV).

God Himself is called our helper, our ezer, the same word
used of the first woman in Genesis 2:18. In the New Testament,
the Holy Spirit is called our Helper, Counselor, and Comforter.
God is our Help. The Holy Spirit is our Helper. When we understand God's role as ezer, we gain needed perspective. God, sovereign Lord of the universe, is our helper, and He created woman to

reflect this aspect of Him. If we hold on to the dominant cultural attitude that being a helper is a substandard identity, we mock the name of God and His character. The role of helper is one He willingly embraces. Hebrews 13:6 says, "The Lord is my helper; I will not fear; what can man do to me?"

Consider God's example as ezer. In Exodus 18:4, God our help "delivered . . . from the sword," defending His own in contrast to attacking or apathetically ignoring the fight altogether. In Psalm 10:14, God our help sees the oppressed and cares for them in their affliction; rather than being indifferent, He is the "helper of the fatherless." In Psalm 20:2 and 33:20, God our help supports, shields, and protects. In Psalm 70:5, God our help delivers from distress. In Psalm 72:12–14, God our help rescues the poor, weak, and needy.

God our help gives a high and worthy example for women to embrace. But His example of help is of one who is in relationship with others, not independent of them. God did not design woman to be a glorified maid, butler, or cook waiting on an order to perform for a master. This is not His relational vision for woman. Instead, He created woman to show compassion, to support, to defend and protect those in her care, to deliver from distress, and to comfort. Women were designed to be conduits of God's grace and strength in their homes, churches, communities, and places of work. Women were designed to be like God Himself.

This description of ezer reflects back on our "serve and protect" language from the creation mandate in Genesis 2. Is a woman's version of this a softer service and a gentler protection than what her male counterpart offers to those with whom he is in relationship? Well, in many circumstances, yes. Womanhood includes a nurturing aspect you can't miss. Yet most of us have either experienced the human version of a mama bear or been one ourselves. Don't get between a mama bear and her cubs, right? I certainly felt this with my children when an angry woman verbally attacked them in a grocery store. But this tendency has risen up in me in other situations too: once when a gang harassed my eighth-grade students on a field trip to the Smithsonian Institute; another time when a much larger dog stalked my small one during a walk. Something stirred in me, and it wasn't unrighteous anger. Because God put a particular nurturing strength in the design of the ezer—don't get between her and those she is called to serve and protect! She will defend and protect in the image of God. We can find great dignity and much to admire in the inherent identity of woman as God created her.

But as beautiful and inspiring as Scripture's use of ezer is in Genesis 2, the Fall (recounted in the next chapter) deeply marred the beauty of God's perfect creation. In Ephesians 1 and 2, the apostle Paul laid out for us all that Christ accomplished for us through His life, death, and resurrection, expounding on it further in Ephesians 3 and 4. Then he opened Ephesians 5 with the amazing phrase, "Therefore be imitators of God." In Christ, you and I have the tool for bridging the vast gulf between our created image in Genesis 2 and the Fall of Genesis 3. Now we can start to reclaim God's likeness in us, and Paul in Ephesians 5 and 6 illustrates what this looks like across the board—for husbands, wives, parents, children, coworkers, bosses, and general relationships within the church. The vision of a woman reflecting God as ezer is no longer a lofty goal marred at the fall of man. We can begin to image Him once more, as we see many sisters in the Scriptures model, looking forward to the Messiah in the Old Testament and looking back to the resurrected Christ in the New Testament.

PURPOSE IN GOD'S LARGER PLAN

A correct understanding of the dignity of a woman's inherent identity as outlined in Genesis 1 and 2 fuels our understanding of woman's purpose in God's larger plan. He tasked her and the man to steward the earth, be fruitful, and multiply humankind. Scripture does not give us examples of how these duties played out in the perfection of the Garden of Eden, but the Bible records many examples of women living their purpose after the Fall, albeit in the context of sinful humanity.

Once we get a vision of what it means to ezer, to strongly help the way God models for us, we start to recognize the purpose and value of that kind of strong help throughout Scripture. We see it in Rahab, Deborah, Ruth, Esther, Mary, Martha, Priscilla, Phoebe, Euodia, and Syntyche.[4] I'd prefer that the Bible spent several chapters all in a row revealing the specific meaning of ezer, complete with detailed instructions on how to live it out. Instead, the Bible gives us vignettes, little glimpses that whet our appetites while leaving much to our imaginations.

Consider Rahab, a foreigner and a prostitute, whose story begins in Joshua 2. At first, she seemed completely alienated from God and His purposes, a shamed woman living far apart from Him. Yet, when the time came, she aided and protected the

Israelite spies, eventually marrying one and giving birth to Boaz, King David's great-grandfather. She served God's larger purposes in her life—purposes that ultimately found their fulfillment well past her death when the Messiah was born of her descendants. She valiantly contributed to something much bigger than herself.

Esther, too, initially seemed alienated from God and His purposes. She was under bondage in a godless kingdom serving a godless king. Yet, like Rahab, Esther put her life on the line to courageously aid in the protection of God's children and His larger plans for Israel.

Priscilla, Phoebe, Euodia, and Syntyche each helped Paul in gospel ministry. Though we are given only brief phrases offering insight into their roles in God's larger purposes, they still help us start to understand what it means to be fruitful in God's image. Such purpose in God's kingdom could in part be the physical fruit of raising children in the faith. It could be spiritual fruit of investing in the lives of others and growing in the fruits of the Spirit ourselves.

Whatever the manifestation of the fruitfulness of these biblical women in God's larger plan, they give us snapshots of what it means to have dominion over the earth, harness the earth, and serve humankind. They did it in their realms of influence, their homes and societies, providing food, clothing, and shelter, and sometimes governance and judgment. Most of all, they gave us an early vision of what it means to help in the likeness of God. God sometimes helps us by providing for our felt needs. We need food, we need clothing, and we need shelter. God's help also comes in the form of our spiritual needs. We need support. We need compassion. We need guidance. We need discipleship. These women evidence aspects of all of these types of help.

IMAGE-BEARING WOMANHOOD IN PRINCIPLE

The Bible gives a little more flesh to these ideas by way of two particular women: the woman of Proverbs 31 and Ruth, the great-grandmother of King David.

Proverbs 31 gives us twenty-two verses illustrating image-bearing womanhood. But unlike the book of Ruth, the description of the honored woman of Proverbs 31 is part of a genre of Scripture called the Wisdom Literature. We need to understand how to read and apply this genre in order to fully appreciate and understand Proverbs 31. This will free us from the misguided way this chapter is sometimes used to demoralize women with often unattainable standards.

It is important to recognize the differences in the wise instructions of Proverbs 31 and, say, the law of the Ten Commandments. One interesting distinction is that the Bible does not give opposite laws or opposite commandments. On the other hand, there *are* opposite proverbs. Consider the secular proverbs of "Look before you leap" and "He who hesitates is lost." We do not see these as contradictory statements but as ones that are appropriate in different circumstances. Proverbs 26:4–5 gives a back-to-back biblical example of seemingly opposite proverbs: "Answer not a fool according to his folly, lest you be like him yourself. Answer a fool according to his folly, lest he be wise in his own eyes." The Bible is not contradicting itself. But like the secular proverbs, it is giving two pieces of wisdom that have application in differing circumstances. Wisdom is wise only when applied correctly in the right situation. A believer reading Proverbs 26, walking with the Holy Spirit, recognizes that there are times when engaging fools verbally will result in becoming like the fools she is trying to rebuke. She also recognizes that sometimes fools need someone to point out their foolishness so they won't believe their own hype. The Holy Spirit is our help in understanding the difference.

You cannot read Proverbs the same way you read the Ten Commandments, yet many Christians fear situational wisdom. Some don't trust others to figure out what applies and how to apply it, so they enforce one-dimensional conclusions that don't allow for the nuances that much of the biblical proverbs offer. The answer to such fear is to apply wisdom in ways that are actually wise through the indwelling Holy Spirit. Paul exhorts us to "walk by the Spirit" in Galatians 5:16 and to "keep in step with the Spirit" in 5:25. It is this pressing into God via the Spirit that equips you and me to apply wisdom in wise ways without fear of moral relativism. The Holy Spirit helps us distinguish principle from application and know what application God has for us, as opposed to what He has for some other person in a different situation.[5]

John recorded these words of Christ in his gospel: "I tell you the truth: it is to your advantage that I go away, for if I do not go away, the Helper will not come to you. But if I go, I will send him to you. And when he comes, he will convict the world concerning sin and righteousness and judgment. . . . When the Spirit of truth comes, he will guide you into all the truth" (16:7–8, 13).

Due in part to the excess of false teachers who abuse the phrase "The Holy Spirit spoke to me" by using it for self-serving purposes, many believers are suspicious of the Holy Spirit. At times in my life, I would have said I'd rather spend three years with Jesus in person as Peter did than twenty years indwelt by the Spirit. Sitting at Jesus's feet seemed, in my head, the ultimate location for the best kind of discipleship. Yet, if we compare Peter after his years in Jesus's presence with Peter after time with the Holy Spirit, we see clearly, as Jesus Himself says, that the latter was better for Peter, resulting in greater growth and maturity in his life. The better ministry of the Holy Spirit in a believer's life is a profound truth Christ Himself taught.

Understanding the difference between wisdom and law, and the role of the Holy Spirit working in us to apply wisdom, consider the woman Proverbs 31 describes. That chapter uses a descriptor for this woman that is closely related to the Hebrew word *ezer.* The phrase is *'ishshah chayil,* or woman of valor, strength, or excellence.[6] As we saw in the Old Testament's use of the word ezer, this woman is characterized by strength: "Strength and dignity are her clothing, and she laughs at the time to come" (verse 25).

There are myriad ways the Proverbs 31 woman's example of strong help shows her purpose in God's larger plan. Her help is demonstrated in her family, it's shown in her work ethic, and it's revealed in her testimony in her community. Proverbs 31 doesn't give us a list of commands for a woman to obey. Instead, it gives us wisdom to apply in our specific circumstances as the Holy Spirit convicts us personally.

IMAGE-BEARING WOMANHOOD IN THE FLESH

While the Proverbs 31 woman is a generic example, a prototype, the Bible uses the same phrase, *'ishshah chayil,* in Ruth 3:11 for another woman in Scripture who lived as a strong helper in tangible ways for God's larger purposes: "My daughter, fear not. I will do for you all you require, for all my people in the city know that you are a woman of strength (worth, bravery, capability)" (AMPC).

The book of Ruth fleshes out strong help with a real-life example: Ruth, the great-grandmother of King David. In fact, in the Hebrew Bible, the book of Ruth immediately follows Proverbs 31, emphasizing her life as a concrete example of that chapter's woman of valor. Throughout her story, Ruth worked hard to provide for herself and her mother-in-law, Naomi, when their safety net fell apart. Boaz, a close relative to Ruth's dead husband, recognized her strength and character, and Naomi told Ruth to pursue him as a husband. Though not fully understanding God's larger purposes for her life, Ruth yielded to the path He had for her nonetheless.

In her faithfulness to Naomi, Ruth took a chance, unsure of the outcome. She risked by moving from her homeland to a country and people she did not know. She risked by putting herself in a vulnerable place to be possibly rejected by Boaz. She listened to Naomi and put her reputation on the line to aid her. Though Proverbs 31 emphasizes valor demonstrated in marriage and motherhood, Boaz recognized Ruth as valiant when she was a barren widow with no prospects of family for the future. Though strong help often finds its manifestation in the womanly roles of wife and mother, it clearly transcends those roles.

As we look at the first woman of Genesis 2, the two specific examples of women of valor from Proverbs 31 and Ruth, and the many vignettes of women strongly helping in God's larger purposes throughout Scripture, an inspiring image emerges. But it is just that—an image, a tselem. It's a rippling reflection of something big and beautiful, something noble and eternal. The reflections are sometimes hard to pin down, but they point to One who is real. They point to God Himself, the best of their actions reflecting something wonderful of Him. God Himself is the North Star for the Bible's vision of women.

How Did It All Go Wrong?

Over the previous two chapters, we've examined the great vision God has for women as His image bearers, serving and protecting His perfect creation. We explored the phrase *strong helper* and saw first God's example of such help and then examples of key women in the Bible. The first two chapters of Genesis give men and women an inspiring goal for their roles as image bearers of God in the world.

Yet, for all the nobility of the commission for man and woman in Genesis 1 and 2, the very next chapters of Scripture leave us raw and wounded, as the reflecting pool of God's image bearers is polluted with foul poison. The stories in Genesis after the Fall reflect little of the noble commission of Genesis 1, with Cain killing Abel, a world destroyed by the Flood, people building a tower to try to reach heaven on their own, and deception and rebellion from the very people on whom God placed His favor.[1] God's own children participated in the foulness of fallen humanity with vigor.

We need redemption.

Redemption: the action of regaining or gaining possession of something in exchange for payment, or clearing a debt.[2]

After studying the beauty of God's creation revealed in Genesis 1 and 2, I long to possess it again. I want to experience the created world as it was before the Fall. But more than that, I want to regain my personhood. I want those around me to get theirs back as well—for all of us to be as God first created us. I want to be the kind of person God set in the garden and tasked with serving and protecting His creation. I want Eden in the world, and I want Eden in myself.

C. S. Lewis gives an intriguing, inspiring vision of such reclaimed image bearing in *The Silver Chair*. Prince Caspian, a principal character in the story of the mythical land of Narnia, has died and is on the other side now. He wants a look back into the former world and wonders to the lion Aslan, who represents God, if his desire to look into the world is wrong, to which Aslan replies, "You cannot want wrong things any more, now that you have died, my son."[3]

Oh, to not want wrong things! I want to live in the perfect creation that God first made and not pollute it with my presence. I long to experience the joys of creation without the pitfalls my fallen nature has added to the landscape. Have you ever considered what life would be like if we lived as God intended in a world that worked as He created it? I long for that deeply, yet it seems an unattainable goal. Heavy darkness in both the national news and the recesses of my private life causes me to despair at times. Yet there is something about Jesus that shines light in these dark places, that restores hope for Eden when we are threatened with resignation over the state of mankind.

But before we explore our hope in Christ for repossessing all that was lost because of the Fall, it is helpful to first understand the Fall itself. God's redeeming grace is meaningless without an understanding of the brokenness of that event. Still, a true understanding of the Fall will kill our hope unless we also understand God's plan to redeem it all.

Grace is meaningless without truth, but that truth will kill you without grace.

MARRED BY THE FALL

Genesis 3 gives insight into the issues underlying much of humanity's struggle after the Fall, particularly as they relate to gender. After Adam and Eve sinned against God, He cursed the serpent who tempted them and then told Adam and Eve the results:

To the woman He said,

"I will greatly multiply
Your pain in childbirth,
In pain you will bring forth children;
Yet your desire will be for your husband,
And he will rule over you."

Then to Adam He said, "Because you have listened to the
voice of your wife, and have eaten from the tree about which
I commanded you, saying, 'You shall not eat from it';

Cursed is the ground because of you;

In toil you will eat of it

All the days of your life;

Both thorns and thistles it shall grow for you;

And you will eat the plants of the field;

By the sweat of your face

You will eat bread,

Till you return to the ground,

Because from it you were taken;

For you are dust,

And to dust you shall return."

(verses 16–19, NASB)

You can see from God's words to Adam that man will clearly struggle with work. Although work was a good part of perfection—a noble calling to steward the world that God gave to mankind—after the Fall it instead became toil. Today work is wearisome, creation no longer cooperating with man but working against him in the quest for fruitfulness.

Women, too, find that their bodies no longer cooperate graciously with the noble calling to be fruitful and multiply with children. Pain and sometimes even death accompany childbirth, and many women's bodies resist even the initial act of conceiving. The Fall profoundly impacted the exterior work of man's hands and the interior work of women's bodies. These are not the only problems with humanity, as women wrestle with work just as men also struggle with their bodies. However, most recognize that these particular battles outlined in Genesis 3 are foundational ones for each gender as a whole.

In terms of interpersonal relationships after the Fall, God's words to Eve give insight to the gender struggle: "I will greatly multiply your pain in childbirth, in pain you will bring forth children; yet your desire will be for your husband, and he will rule over you" (verse 16, NASB). The Bible offers only a quick description of the consequences of the Fall in this passage. We are left again to look at the definition of the Hebrew words and infer from other verses that reflect on them exactly what God is communicating here. The two words I want to focus on in this passage are *desire* and *rule.* There is something negative in the way the Bible uses both of these words in this verse. The Hebrew word for "rule," *mashal,* can be translated "gain control" or "master."[4] It is a different word from the one used in the command to have dominion over the earth, yet it seems to have a similar meaning. Man and woman were commanded by God to have dominion over creation together. But this use of *rule* after the Fall reflects something different, something that isn't as it should be. This rule, man's over woman in the marriage and family relationship, is a warping away from God's intended purpose.

In Ephesians 5, you can see redemption of the image of God in man in particular when the apostle Paul exhorts husbands to love their wives as Christ loved the church. There is a profound difference between the oppressive rule of man over woman predicted in Genesis 3 (and well evidenced in our world) and the sacrificial headship in marriage envisioned in

Paul's instructions in Ephesians 5, which I will unpack more in chapters 8 and 9.

It doesn't take long while scouring modern news outlets to see that apart from Christ, Genesis 3–type male rule still exists throughout our world, sometimes very close to home. Though women have made great advances, particularly in Western cultures, in gaining rights over the past hundred years, men still overtly rule over women in oppressive ways in many countries. In Saudi Arabia, for instance, women gained the right to vote in 2015 but still need the permission of a male authority figure to work or travel.[5] In China, there were thirty-three million more men than women in the last census due to sex-selective abortions.[6] In some cultures, the words "It's a girl" can be a death sentence, as boys are favored to the point that girls' lives are discarded.[7] According to Genesis 3, this oppression and devaluing of women, particularly in families and homes, is a result of the Fall.

There is a parallel complicating issue presented in this verse, as Scripture uses another word in Genesis 3:16 to describe the fundamental struggles of gender after the Fall: *desire.* What does the Bible mean when it says that the woman will desire the man? The Hebrew word for "desire," *tshuwqah,* is used only two other times in the Old Testament. Genesis 4:7 says, "If you do well, will you not be accepted? And if you do not do well, sin is crouching at the door. Its *desire* is for you, but you must rule over it," and Song of Solomon 7:10 says, "I am my beloved's, and his *desire* is for me."

Several historic interpretations exist for the phrase "Your desire will be for your husband" from Genesis 3:16 (NASB). Some believed that it represented a sexual desire. But its use in Genesis 4:7 seems to contradict that supposition. Some believed it meant turning, in this case that the woman turns toward her husband but is oppressed in return. Others in church history believed it meant simply desire, craving, or strong longing. Those last two meanings are similar and fit all three uses in the Old Testament.

In the 1970s, some first suggested that this desire referred to a woman's longing to dominate her husband.[8] Although that use of the word might fit Genesis 4:7,* it does not fit Song of Solomon 7:10. The standard definition of this word in Hebrew lexicons and concordances is "longing" or "craving,"[9] which, again, fits all three of the instances in the Old Testament. Viewed in this light, the phrase in Genesis 3:16 reflects a desire for the man that now results in frustration and even abuse. *Just as the man was created to work the ground but is now frustrated in his attempts, the woman was created to help the man but is frustrated in her attempts.* How do both men and women respond apart from Christ to such frustration? For women, this desire can turn into an inappropriate craving bordering on idolatry for something from the man that only God can now

---

* It's important to know that translators debate Genesis 4:7 as well as Genesis 3:16. The pronoun in the Hebrew of 4:7 is masculine, but *sin* in the previous sentence is feminine. John Calvin thought that the pronoun instead referred to Abel (His desire is for you, but you will rule over him), which would fit the masculine pronoun and parallel more closely with the issue in 3:16.

provide her. The issue may be best understood by making the simple substitution of God for her husband. Her desire must be for her God. She should turn toward Him in her need. Instead, her longings are frustrated as she turns toward one who cannot satisfy the needs of her soul that resulted from the fall of man.

Psalm 73 talks of similar desire after the Fall correctly directed toward God. In that chapter, the psalmist recounts his great emotional battle, a good summary of the overall struggle of life in a fallen world. The wicked were flourishing, those who followed God were mocked, and the psalmist seemed on the verge of losing his faith. Then he entered the presence of God, and the life of faith began to make sense again. The grand climax of this psalm is found in verses 25–26: "Whom have I in heaven but you? And there is nothing on earth that I desire besides you. My flesh and my heart may fail, but God is the strength of my heart and my portion forever."

Nothing on earth can replace what God gives to sustain our hearts. In contrast, Genesis 3:16 presents us a picture of a woman, created to be a strong helper to the man, who instead turns toward the man for emotional and spiritual affirmation and provision that he can't provide in his own frustrated state working unfruitful ground. God alone is the source that can meet these desires. Her heart will be restless until it again finds its rest in God.[10]

In this sense, the man's root problem from the Fall leads to a frustrated idolatry of work, while the woman's leads to a frustrated idolatry of man.

HEAR ME OUT

My analysis of this root problem may sound offensive, but stay with me.* The real offense is not pointing out that such idolatry of man exists but rather the many ways our culture exploits it. I've certainly experienced this. Have you? At various points in my life, I looked to men to meet needs in my heart they could not provide on their best days emotionally, spiritually, or physically. Once these men disappointed me, instead of recognizing my sovereign, compassionate, and wise Father as the One I should seek, I looked within myself for emotional, spiritual, and physical independence. And how much harder it is for women to navigate this in cultures where oppression is government sanctioned! How do women face this need in their hearts when it is compounded by utter dependence on men for physical safety and financial support in countries where they cannot even vote?

Even in Western cultures with greater freedom for women, this turning toward men who exploit in return is clearly evident. Media, in particular, is full of examples of women actively participating in their own exploitation out of a misplaced need for affirmation or approval from men, along with the men who willingly take advantage of them for financial gain

---

* Though my analysis here sounds particularly negative concerning men, remember that this reflects our needs and tendencies apart from Christ after the Fall. In later chapters we will explore God's redemption of men and manhood. God's sons are necessary for His work, and they deeply bless the women in their lives when conformed to the image of Christ.

or sexual satisfaction. Yet our Western culture has also adopted reactions against it. Women often recognize weakness or strength among themselves by how they react when men fail them. The perceived strong feminist woman is the one who does not need men. The perceived weak woman is the one who continues to follow abusive men around like a starving puppy.

Is there a better way? Is our only hope for coexistence between the genders to develop coping mechanisms for restraining male oppression and pursuing female independence? These types of activities do not get us back to the garden. They don't set the broken bone that it may heal. They instead bind the broken bone out of place.

THE ANSWER IN CHRIST

In Christ, we have a new and different way. Even before God gave the sad consequences of the Fall to man and woman in Genesis 3, He first announced the coming reconciliation: "He shall bruise your head," God said to the serpent in verse 15. One was coming who would give Satan a massive blow to the head.

In chapter 1, we saw in the discussion of the scarlet thread how the rest of the Old Testament then points to Jesus's coming in the New. Jesus came, He lived, He died, and He was resurrected. Later, New Testament writers fleshed out from multiple angles what Christ had done for God's children. In terms of Jesus's fulfillment of the Old Testament sacrificial system, consider what the author of Hebrews teaches us.

Since we have confidence to enter the holy places by the
blood of Jesus, by the new and living way that he opened for
us through the curtain, that is, through his flesh, and since
we have a great priest over the house of God, let us draw
near with a true heart in full assurance of faith. (10:19–22)

Let us then with confidence draw near to the throne of
grace, that we may receive mercy and find grace to help in
time of need. (4:16)

Take a moment to consider what these passages refer to. In
the Old Testament, the temple consisted of an outer courtyard, in
which the common people were allowed, and an inner sanctuary,
called the Holy of Holies, in which only the priests were allowed.
The Holy of Holies housed the ark of the covenant, God's symbolic presence with His people. A thick veil stood between the
Holy of Holies and the area where the priests were allowed. Once
a year, the high priest entered the Holy of Holies with severe restrictions. He had to bring a blood sacrifice. He needed to be puri-
fied. Even after these preparations, tradition taught that the other
priests attached a rope to his ankle so they could pull him out in
the event he entered unworthily, and God struck him dead.

At Christ's death on the cross, He cried out at the climactic
moment of His sacrifice, "It is finished" (John 19:30). Matthew
27:51 says, "At that moment the curtain of the temple was torn in
two from top to bottom" (NIV). The heavy, thick barrier between
the children of God and His symbolic presence was ripped apart.
The doorway to God's presence was opened wide.

This access to God is key to the redemption Christ brings. It is key to reclaiming our part in God's commission to women in the garden. After their sin, Adam and Eve were banished from the garden and estranged from the God with whom they had enjoyed a free relationship. But Christ tore down the barrier between us and God.

In terms of the particular struggles outlined in Genesis 3:16, the woman redeemed by Christ is restored as God's honored daughter with full access to the King of kings. Her needs can now be met through the freedom she has to boldly and confidently approach her Father in heaven to ask for help. Because she finds grace and mercy in her time of need, she can then be God's image-bearing strong helper to others in theirs. God pours grace into her, equips her, and satisfies her emotional, spiritual, and physical needs. Only then can she stay engaged with the man as the helper God created her to be. Woman's problem is not her strong longings, or desires. The issue is whom she sees as the correct object of them.

"There is nothing on earth that I desire besides you," the psalmist said (Psalm 73:25). But he said it only after he'd entered the sanctuary of God (see verse 17). This access to God that you and I have freely through Jesus is key to the good news of redemption. This access to Him where we find grace and mercy in our time of need is the singular antidote to the frustrated desires predicted for the woman in Genesis 3.

WHAT DO GRACE AND MERCY LOOK LIKE?

What does this access to God accomplish for us? What does the author of Hebrews mean when he says we can find grace and mercy for our needs by availing ourselves of this access? And what do these things look like in tangible terms?

Second Corinthians 9:8 says, "God is able to make all grace abound to you, so that having all sufficiency in all things at all times, you may abound in every good work." The benefit is described in this verse with the word *sufficiency,* which means having what is needed—having adequate provision and supplies. In a world of people and situations that consistently miss the mark of God's perfection and all He intended us to be, when we avail ourselves of our access to God through Christ, we find sufficient supplies for this season.[11]

We have something that bridges the gap between the godly longings set in our hearts in Eden and our fallen reality. It is the gospel, the good news of this access we have to God through Christ that the Hebrews passages described to us. This good news is the bridge that makes a way for us to return to Eden, live in light of God's commission to man and woman, and once again be "imitators of God" (Ephesians 5:1). God has done something through the life, death, and resurrection of Christ by which He is able to make "all grace abound" to us. Through Christ, we are abundantly supplied for every good, image-bearing work to which He has called us.

Although the gospel is a bigger concept than one chapter in a book this size can adequately address, I hope to present enough material that we understand the gospel as the foundation for applying passages on womanhood to our lives. What did Christ's life and death bring that empowers you and me to live confidently as God's strong helpers in a broken world?

I grow year by year in understanding how the gospel truly changes everything in my life. I came to understand in my youth the good news that Jesus paid my debt to God. But I was well into adulthood before I realized how Scripture also speaks of God's lavish grace credited to my account. Second Corinthians 5:21 says, "For our sake he made him to be sin who knew no sin, so that in him we might become the righteousness of God." This is the Great Exchange. I had an infinite debt to God. I was, by nature, deserving of His wrath, dead in my sins, and unable to save myself (see Ephesians 2:8–9). I have benefited greatly from Christ's death (known as *penal substitution* in theological circles), which paid that debt on my behalf. But I also have benefited greatly from Jesus's life, a doctrine called *imputed righteousness.*

Consider an inmate who has received a long sentence that he rightly deserves. Though he has no hope of freeing himself, his record is suddenly marked "Paid in full!" By the mercy of the judge and sacrifice of another, he walks out of jail a free man. While he may be momentarily grateful that he no longer owes a debt to society, he faces a long, hard road. He has no money for food. He cannot pay a taxi to take him home (if he even has somewhere to go). Unless someone on the outside is waiting to help him, he cannot afford a motel room. His best chances are to sleep under a bridge and steal food wherever he can find it. In this scenario, he is set up to return to a life of crime. His only hope is to pull himself up by the bootstraps. But pitfalls surround him and he has virtually no safety net. This illustrates the difference between a view of the gospel that ends with penal substitution and one that also strongly embraces imputed righteousness.

In the book of Ephesians, the apostle Paul emphasizes both penal substitution and imputed righteousness in the good news of Jesus. He starts in Ephesians 1, not with the payment of sin but with God's lavish grace. In Christ, he says, we are blessed "with every spiritual blessing" (verse 3). He goes through those blessings in detail, praying at the end of chapter 1 that the Ephesian believers would understand the wealth of this inheritance, this imputed righteousness, and the great power at work on their behalf. Then in Ephesians 2, Paul teaches that the people were dead in their sins, by nature deserving of God's wrath and alienated from Him. Perhaps Paul saw the need to follow the order of Genesis 3, which predicted the coming Savior before listing the consequences of the fall of man. Paul stresses the positive promise of spiritual blessing before examining the negative problem of the Fall that the promises of grace address.

Redemption isn't completed simply by Christ's payment for our sins. In Him, we also have an abundant surplus in our account because God sees you and me wearing Christ's "robe of righteousness" (Isaiah 61:10). If we are believers in Christ, we are now righteous, but not by works of our own. God has poured this righteousness on us by His mercy and grace, and we can rest in it. You and I are prisoners set free from our well-deserved sentence who now have the spiritual resources of children of the King.

EQUIPPED IN HIM

The call given to us in Genesis 1 and 2 to serve and protect God's creation is no longer an unattainable ideal. We can be strong helpers who are fruitful and multiply—the noble commission spoken over the first man and woman and then redeemed by Jesus as He spoke the Great Commission to His disciples before He returned to heaven. These are the very works of Ephesians 2:10 that God prepared in advance for us to do and that 2 Corinthians 9:8 teaches we are sufficiently equipped by God's grace now to accomplish. This is our role in God's kingdom come, as we die more and more to sin and live more and more in righteousness.

Through Genesis 1 and 2, you were given a grand commission to bear God's image into the world. Despite the fall of man and your own personal sin, your dignity was restored when Jesus commissioned His disciples and us once again to bear God's image into the world. You are now equipped for this work by accessing God through Christ, where you'll find great grace that enables you to do the work to which He has called you. Paul exhorts us, "Be renewed in the spirit of your minds, and . . . put on the new self, created after the likeness of God in true righteousness and holiness. . . . Therefore be imitators of God, as beloved children" (Ephesians 4:23–24; 5:1). The circle is completed, and we are able once more, through Christ, to be the image bearers of God He created us to be in perfection.

This long story of Scripture that culminates in the Great Commission of Jesus Christ both inspires and equips me as God's image bearer during my earthly life. But it also transcends my lifetime, which leads us to the next chapter.

Is It Going to Get Better?

The first four chapters of this book set up a foundation to answer the question of its title, "Is the Bible good for women?" We have examined God's purposes for man and woman in perfection, the ways the Fall warped us away from that purpose, and the hope we have that God is reclaiming this image in us through Christ's sacrifice for us on the cross. We did all this after establishing a Jesus-centered understanding of reading Scripture. With this foundation, we are ready to unpack this question of the goodness of the Bible for women.

What I mean when I ask if the Bible is good for women is if an orthodox understanding of the Bible, a reading and understanding of Scripture that has held steady over thousands of years, one understood through Jesus as He instructed His disciples on the road to Emmaus, is good for women. Peaks and valleys of interpretation have shown up season by season in the church, and applications of such orthodox understanding of Scripture have also waxed and waned over the years based on culture and history. I am concerned here with the long views that have persevered throughout church history in creeds and confessions, and a church-wide understanding of the actual text itself rather than individual or group application, which can vary significantly by generation and culture.

Many modern books on the Bible and women do not hold to an orthodox view of the Bible. They suggest that the answer to the question of the Bible's goodness for women is "No!" They then introduce new understandings of the Bible regarding women — understandings with no history in the church. With such an approach, though, we also lose many other orthodox teachings from Scripture that are deep and meaningful. In my opinion, God has given us a better way to interact with His Word.

One applicable doctrine to this discussion is called the perspicuity, or clarity, of Scripture. The question is if the church can and should accept Scripture at face value. Does it mean what it says, particularly applied to the church's understanding of salvation? This doctrine arose as a rejection of the idea that people needed a priest to retranslate Scripture for them (or add to it something it did not say) in order for them to understand the gospel and salvation. After the Reformation, believers became convinced that the Bible was clear enough on the gospel and Jesus that even the unlearned could understand it. Part of the question for this book is if we can have a similar approach to the clarity of Scripture and its trustworthiness when it comes to the Bible's words on gender.

Do we need to retranslate the Bible for it to be good for women? Do we need to write off parts of it that have been traditionally understood in ways that seem limiting to women? Are women blessed or harmed by reading, understanding, and obeying Scripture as it has been handed down for generations?

It makes complete sense to me that women struggle to believe that a book thousands of years old is good for the modern woman. Doesn't the progress in Western cultures on women's issues make the Bible's instructions pertaining to women outdated? Some who speak about this tension suggest that, when you boil it all down, we should disregard the Bible altogether, which is a consistent way to approach it, even if I disagree with that conclusion! We are self-deceived if we think we can pick and choose which parts of Scripture we will obey based on our own likes and dislikes. Yet I understand why someone would throw the entire Bible out before believing that some parts were good and some were bad, that some were trustworthy and some were not.

But what if we don't pick and choose from the Bible ourselves and instead let Scripture do it for us? We circle back to the principle I've discussed in several chapters: that the Bible is the best commentary on itself. We are going to deal with this principle from multiple angles in various chapters of this book because it is the most important concept for determining if the Bible is good for women.

THE BIBLE DECODES THE BIBLE

The Bible teaches us how to receive different parts of itself for today, and this is key to understanding our Bibles so that we can answer the central question of this book. For this chapter, I want to emphasize again the basis of a Jesus-centered understanding of Scripture.

First, Jesus fulfilled and did not erase the Law. What the Law was attempting to do and did inadequately, Jesus did perfectly. Matthew 5:17 says, "Do not think that I have come to abolish the Law or the Prophets; I have not come to abolish them but to fulfill them." We no longer are constrained by the Law or enact the penalties of the Law, but we should continue to value it for what it teaches of God's character and values. We deal with this in depth in chapter 7.

Second, the problem with sin and the resolution that Jesus brings is the central message of the Old Testament. We learned this from Jesus's words on the road to Emmaus. Remember Luke 24:25–27? Jesus said, "'O foolish ones, and slow of heart to believe all that the prophets have spoken! Was it not necessary that the Christ should suffer these things and enter into his glory?' And beginning with Moses and all the Prophets, he interpreted to them in all the Scriptures the things concerning himself."

When we let the Bible explain the Bible to us, we are equipped with better tools for deciding if the Bible is good for women.

The next part of the question is whether the Bible as a whole is good. But we must first examine what we mean by *good*. That is the thousand-dollar question. We need to make sure we are using God's definition of *good* and not our limited earthly one. His good tends to be slightly different from ours. His good breaks into the present but it is also about the future. As Paul said in 1 Corinthians 15:19, "If in Christ we have hope in this life only, we are of all people most to be pitied." The Bible gives us hope of something better to come, and that oddly leads to quite a bit of good now. It's a different kind of good, but it's also the best kind.

THE BEST KIND OF GOOD

Consider the interaction in the Gospels between Jesus and the rich young ruler, a seeker wrestling with His claims. This exchange gives us insight into God's version of good. One might think Jesus would have eased the tone of His message to draw to faith this young man who was clearly seeking truth—that Jesus would have lured him in with some promise of earthly goodness. But He took a different tactic, painting in stark terms what following Him would mean for this man.

> As he was setting out on his journey, a man ran up and knelt before him and asked him, "Good Teacher, what must I do to inherit eternal life?" And Jesus said to him, "Why do you call me good? No one is good except God alone. You know the commandments: 'Do not murder, Do not commit adultery, Do not steal, Do not bear false witness, Do not defraud, Honor your father and mother.'" And he said to him, "Teacher, all these I have kept from my youth." And Jesus, looking at him, loved him, and said to him, "You lack one thing: go, sell all that you have and give to the poor, and you will have treasure in heaven; and come, follow me." Disheartened by the saying, he went away sorrowful, for he had great possessions. (Mark 10:17–22)

Jesus didn't give an easy answer to this young man, but He did give one that was consistent with His message throughout the

New Testament: if you want to find your life, you must first lose it. He spoke to this man of loss, and it seemed a weight this man could not endure. He left Jesus sorrowful; God's call was too heavy to bear. Yet Jesus always called His disciples through loss to a reward. To this young man, Jesus promised treasure in heaven. Jesus's call was very much a good call with a good outcome, but this young man was too bound to his earthly possessions to perceive it. God's good is a counterintuitive good from our earthly perspective, but I emphasize again that it is the best kind of good.

When I first read this interaction between Jesus and the young ruler, I was struck by the juxtaposition of Jesus's love for this man and the message He spoke to him. But Jesus did not tell him an unloving thing. Jesus told him a true thing, and we fool ourselves regarding the nature of genuine love when we believe that it would be better served with a lie. A lying love is a short-sighted love.

Out of love for him, Jesus told him, in essence, that he must value following Jesus above his possessions, that faith in Jesus would mean choices that don't fit an earthly ideal of security or responsible behavior. In Jesus's service, he would have to deny himself and take up his cross. What a hard path! But this man would not be left to do this on his own. Consider the description of Jesus in Hebrews 12:2: "The founder and perfecter of our faith, who for the joy that was set before him endured the cross, despising the shame, and is seated at the right hand of the throne of God."

When I read this verse, I envision Jesus looking through a door into a room filled with the worst kind of pain and shame:

what He experienced on the cross. Yet through a door on the other side of the room, He can see through the pain and shame of the cross to the purest kind of joy and goodness. He walked through that room of pain and shame, enduring the worst evil, and then through the door on the other side, where He now sits in peace and joy at the right hand of His Father. And according to Hebrews 12:2, we are to look to Him. He is our inspiration for and example of something God calls us to here on earth.

God's Version of Good

Joy is available. The best kind of goodness exists at God's feet in His throne room. There we can find joy, and peace, and satisfaction. But God's version of good is not like the temporary earthly joy of money and nice houses that some religious figures offer their followers. It is not self-actualization ("the achievement of one's full potential through creativity, independence, spontaneity, and a grasp of the real world"[1]) in the present. It's not an earthly "Be all you can be."

No, God's version of good sets such a view of the fulfillment of our potential on its side.

Jesus *loved* this young ruler He said this hard thing to. The description of Jesus's interaction with this man has the language of goodness—of a desire for the best for someone. But we clearly see that Jesus's idea of the loving, best direction for this young man challenged the man's own view of good. He left disappointed, unable to comprehend such an invitation from Jesus being worth the cost.

Jesus's invitation was not to self-actualization, but it was not to self-flagellation, either. We are not simply to deny ourselves or beat ourselves up. Those who lose their lives will *find them,* and the implication is that what they find is very much worth the pursuit (see Matthew 10:39). God's good is the kind of sustaining, life-giving good that feeds our souls. Ultimately, God's call to this young man, and to us, is about finding the best kind of good. It is about finding true life, not restricting it.

Maybe you get where I am going. Understanding the goodness of the Bible requires a long view through the dark room Jesus endured to the joy and goodness on the far side. Eschatology is the Christian study of the last days—how things end on the far side of God's story. There is great debate about how exactly those things work out in terms of rapture, resurrection, new heaven, and new earth. Yet the long conviction of the church throughout the centuries is that it ends well for believers. In the end, God's kingdom is fully realized and there is a new heaven and a new earth where we live in peace and joy with God as He first created us to do. God's Word to us is a long book extended over a long period of time that reflects an even longer story to be fulfilled in eternity.

This eternal good story must be the stream that feeds the reservoir that is our understanding of our earthly temporary good.

FLESHING OUT A GOOD LIFE

Remember Joseph's story in Genesis 37–50? Joseph's jealous brothers sold him into slavery. He was accused of rape and thrown into prison, where he languished for years. As we've seen, he was finally promoted to second-in-command in Egypt, and he provided food for his family when they were about to be destroyed by starvation.

Many love Joseph's story because God worked an end to his life that gave purpose to his years of suffering and struggle in Egypt. The earthly resolution in Joseph's lifetime to the long estrangement from his family gives us hope to endure our own suffering, as it should. Maybe after decades of endurance in suffering we, too, will see the clouds pull back as God gives us a glimpse of His good purposes in our lifetime. Joseph's story encourages us to reflect on a God who turns circumstances others use against us for good in our lives and in the lives of those we love (see Genesis 50:20).

Yet when Joseph is commended for his faith in Hebrews 11, it isn't because he endured in jail or provided food for his family. He wasn't commended for running from sin with Potiphar's wife or enduring in faith until he saw his father and little brother again. He was commended because, at his death, he instructed his children to take his bones with them when they entered the Promised Land: "By faith Joseph, at the end of his life, made mention of the exodus of the Israelites and gave directions concerning his bones" (verse 22).

This is profound! Scripture praises Joseph for his last act, asking his relatives to dig up and carry his bones with them to the Promised Land when God finally gave it to them. He was looking past his death to God's purposes beyond his lifetime. He believed in something that transcended his earthly years and gave purpose to his struggle more than even the earthly resolution with his family. Joseph's life was empowered by his eschatology—his faith in God's plan beyond his lifetime for how He would reconcile events for eternity.

Joseph's convictions of *eternal good* settled him. They gave meaning to his earthly suffering. They equipped him for the flourishing life God had for him. They equipped him to endure some very dark places. These convictions equipped him to recognize the beauty of his reconciliation with his brothers as well.

WITNESSES TO ULTIMATE GOOD

Many questioning the goodness of the Bible don't value an answer that takes an eternal view. We use phrases such as *human flourishing* or again *self-actualization,* rooted in the here and now. But I submit that we can gain no understanding of either biblical manhood or biblical womanhood without an eschatological view of gender, a view that extends past our lifetimes to God's end goal for humanity. Even the creation mandate to steward the earth is best understood with an awareness of end times. According to Romans 8:22–24, creation groans with our waiting for God to right all that is wrong in the world. We steward it now in preparation for this end.

Hebrews 11 calls us to a faith that believes that God rewards those who diligently seek Him (see verse 6). But I note that those in history who were applauded for that kind of faith, believing in God's good rewards, were also sometimes tortured, mocked, flogged, imprisoned, stoned, sawed in two, and killed by the sword (see verses 35–37). Hebrews 11 describes them at times as "destitute, afflicted, mistreated" (verse 37).

God's goodness is very good, and it is very good on earth, but there is a clear element of it that includes dying to self that we might become alive to God to experience it. Through death to self, we find flourishing life. The good that God wants us to seek is counterintuitive—a good with a long view of life on earth and eternity future. Nevertheless, it is still very, very good.

COMMUNAL GOOD VERSUS INDIVIDUAL GOOD

"It is not good that the man should be alone" (Genesis 2:18). From these earliest words of God over humanity, we see that even in perfection, one by himself could not attain the full good that God intended for him. God's vision for our good is communal. Over and over again in the Bible, the good of the many feeds individual good in God's kingdom. God ordained community in the Garden of Eden. He made both man and woman and commanded them to fill the earth with others like them. The flourishing of communities is necessary for the flourishing of the individual. The good of God's kingdom community precedes the good of the individuals within it. But that eventually leads to eternal self-actualization, if Scripture is to be believed. Our earthly sanctification as individuals in the community leads to a corporate church that is glorious (see Ephesians 5:26–27). And a church that is glorious in the image of God blesses its individual parts!

I submit to you that the Bible is very good for women, but we have to be precise in how we define *good*. To be consistent with

Scripture, we have to face a "lose your life to find it" kind of good. We have to decide if a long view of good with eternal promise is enough to endure perceived losses in the temporal. We also have to accept a communal good that sometimes calls for individual sacrifices for the good of others. We have reached the fork in the road that turns many away from the Bible altogether. If the Bible isn't going to lift them up this week or month with earthly, individual self-actualization, then it is not worth pursuing. That, friend, is not the kind of faith that God commends in Hebrews 11.

This long, communal view is deeply relevant to all of us in the body of Christ seeking to live God's commission in Jesus's name. For our purposes in this book, it is particularly relevant to women seeking to understand a good Bible that teaches us God's plan to use women in noble ways in His kingdom. This world is not our home. Its earthly riches are not our eternal ones. We are renters here: stewards of God's creation awaiting our permanent place in it in eternity. And we steward His creation in cohort with our fellow image bearers. These truths are unmistakable in the stories of men and women of strength in the Old Testament. This is how people of faith, who plowed forward through hardship in light of God's commission, thought of their lives. Such eschatology feeds our understanding of God's good plan for women in Scripture.

LONG-TERM AND COMMUNAL GOOD

Many questioning the goodness of the Bible *for women* don't value an answer that takes an eternal or communal view of good.

I believe that God's goodness to women through Scripture is good for women now, but I believe it is also good for women for eternity. This understanding challenges us to seek an *eternal* answer to the question in the title of this book. Is the Bible good for women? If good for women is limited to earthly self-actualization, then the good we seek is not consistent with the good the Bible offers.

Such an earthbound view of goodness has no room for martyrs—those who are put to death for their faith—or those who die looking to Jesus from their cancer beds. An earthly view of goodness might allow for temporary suffering: for children who get well and broken bones that can be reset, for the cancer that goes into remission, or for the marriage that is restored. That view of goodness might still value the testimony of Corrie ten Boom, whose book *The Hiding Place* details her imprisonment in a Nazi concentration camp during World War II. Corrie was eventually freed and spent the rest of her life giving testimony of God's watchful care of her during her imprisonment. But what do we do with her sister, who died at the worst of it? Of her sister's death, Corrie wrote, "There lay Betsie, her eyes closed as if in sleep, her face full and young. The care lines, the grief lines, the deep hollows of hunger and disease were simply gone. In front of me was the Betsie of Haarlem, happy and at peace. Stronger! Freer! This was the Betsie of heaven, bursting with joy and health."[2]

There is a good that Rahab, Tamar, Hagar, Joseph, and Esther understood from far off. Corrie ten Boom and her sister understood this. Dietrich Bonhoeffer did too as he walked, praying the psalms, to his death at the hands of Nazis. Believers who persevere in belief through the pain of long-term suffering understand a good that is better than our limited earthly ideas of human flourishing—ideas that make the prosperity gospel so popular even though it fails its followers again and again. In Romans 8:18, Paul writes, "I consider that the sufferings of this present time are not worth comparing with the glory that is to be revealed to us." In 2 Corinthians 1:5, he says, "As we share abundantly in Christ's sufferings, so through Christ we share abundantly in comfort too." We need a biblical understanding of suffering to understand the good of God's promises, both here on earth and in eternity future.

I note that other religions call their adherents to a similar long-term view of far-off rewards, and that this view is often a fundamental conviction of those carrying out suicidal killings of others. At first my reaction is to reject a long view of eternity that gives purpose to self-sacrifice like martyrdom, for I have witnessed how groups have used such a view to wreak terror on many. Yet in the Bible, the motivation for self-sacrifice is not to take life for God's kingdom but to give it. Esther laid her life on the line to intercede for the lives of God's people, not to destroy the king's court. Joseph's sacrifice served to save others. Jesus's did too. They were willing to sacrifice their short-term personal good for the greater good of their brothers and sisters—the communal good. Communal good and eternal good are foundations of a biblical view of goodness in the kingdom of God.

ETERNAL GOOD APPLIED TO WOMEN

How does a long view of God's eternal purposes give us the right lens through which to view Scripture about women? I would argue that a case can be made for a short view of goodness regarding the Bible's instructions to women—that there is much value for our lifetimes in the instructions of the Bible to women, particularly around sexual ethics, faithfulness to vows, and maintaining relationships in the home, which are the communal good that aids individual flourishing as well. But we often overemphasize the value of obedience in our lifetimes, resulting in people who turn away from such obedience when they do not see the good result in their own temporal experiences the way Christian leaders presented it in youth group. Their naive expectations of how life would turn out if they obeyed God and pursued righteousness are turned on their head. Without a theology of suffering and a long view of God's goodness around their story, they fall away from their childhood understanding of Scripture and maybe the faith altogether.

Instead, the long story of Scripture presents to us a better, deeper way. Much of the Bible's inherent goodness for women (and men) is tied to God's eternal purposes that infuse the highs and lows of our earthly reality with supernatural import. Tamar, Rahab, and Ruth are three Old Testament women whose stories speak to this truth. In Genesis 38, Tamar posed as a whore to get her father-in-law to impregnate her to continue the line of Judah since he refused to give her his son as the Law later required in this circumstance (see Deuteronomy 25:5). Christians versed in Scripture today understand the phrase *the line of Judah* to indicate Jesus's noble birth line that confirmed His place as the son of Abraham and the rightful Messiah (see Matthew 1:1). But for Tamar, her place in the line of Judah likely didn't feel that honorable, for she played a prostitute to get her father-in-law, Judah himself, to continue the line through her, though at the time she may have simply wanted a legal heir. Though Judah eventually recognized his sin against Tamar and commended her as more righteous than he for insisting he continue the line through her, it isn't until the genealogy of Jesus that we first hear her name spoken with honor for her place in His lineage.

Rahab is a similar figure. Almost every reference to her in the book of Joshua refers to her as a prostitute. Rahab the prostitute. The prostitute Rahab. She was rescued from the destruction of Jericho, yet the end of her story in Joshua is unremarkable. She and her family were safe—the end. Again, it isn't until the genealogy of Jesus that her name shows up, this time as mother of a noble character of the Old Testament, Boaz. And then Hebrews 11 commends her for her faith, and her story breaks out in glory (see verse 31).

Ruth's story is similar. She suffered on earth and enjoyed a measure of earthly redemption in her story after marrying Boaz and giving birth to their son, who would be the grandfather of King David. Yet, like Tamar and Rahab, it isn't for another millennium, until Jesus breaks onto the scene, that we see the true eternal import of her story. As one writer put it, "Messiah [came] not in spite of their painful circumstances, but through them."[3]

Consider for a moment what it was like for each of these women to live without our perspective today of what was eventually accomplished through them.

Consider too how they feel about their suffering today. Are they resentful for their suffering on earth? "Well, they're dead!" you might say. But faith in Christ says they are not. Faith in Christ and the Bible says that they are still living and that their eternal perspective now is informed by perfect truth. They no longer see through a glass darkly. But what's notable about their lives is that they trusted when through a glass darkly was the only view they had (see 1 Corinthians 13:12). They could see only a limited portion of what was going on, and they participated anyway, trusting in God long term even though they had not even begun to understand all God was going to do through their direct descendants. They found the ultimate self-actualization, the ultimate realization of their full potential, but no one else recognized it during their lives the way we see it years afterward:

> These all died in faith, not having received the things
> promised, but having seen them and greeted them from
> afar, and having acknowledged that they were strangers
> and exiles on the earth. For people who speak thus make it
> clear that they are seeking a homeland. If they had been
> thinking of that land from which they had gone out, they
> would have had opportunity to return. But as it is, they
> desire a better country, that is, a heavenly one. Therefore
> God is not ashamed to be called their God, for he has
> prepared for them a city. (Hebrews 11:13–16)

THE DIFFERENCE THE GOSPEL MAKES

What separates this long view in Christ from a works-based religion that offers a greater reward in eternity because of sacrifice on earth? Only the gospel. Note that with Rahab in particular, she was invited into God's purposes while she was practicing sin for which the Law said she should be stoned. She was so heavily involved in this sin that it had become her identity in that culture: Rahab the prostitute. When her sin was ever before her, God called her to Himself and then used her in valiant ways. Who knows exactly what Rahab understood of God at that moment beyond the fact that the people who were called His children were taking over her land? But the Hebrews 11 passage that commends her begins by saying that the faith that pleases God consists of the belief that He exists and that He rewards those who diligently seek Him (see verses 1, 6). Whatever Rahab believed in the time of Joshua about God and His purposes, God poured His grace on her while she was still a sinner. He drew her to Himself, and He used her in His purposes by His grace, for she certainly wasn't righteous by the Law's standards.

Tamar played a harlot, while Rahab was one in truth. Ruth was simply a heathen from a foreign land with a foreign god. These three women were outcasts who show up in the lineage of the Messiah, God Himself. They point to something beautiful about the God who reaches into our lives while we are still sinners and creates something beautiful for His eternal purposes—something *good*.

Jesus's conversation with the rich young ruler in Mark 10 resonates with me. I appreciate it because, like the hard but loving ultimatum Jesus gave him, the Bible's commission to women (and men) is often one of self-sacrifice and delayed gratification. Jesus's words to that young man force me to distinguish between earthly human flourishing and eternal human flourishing—between a prosperity gospel with a "Be all that you can be on earth" end goal and self-sacrifice in service of the mission of Another. The stories of women in Scripture, read thousands of years after their death, inspire me, too, to give myself to something that transcends my lifetime. And that vision infuses the most mundane of earthly sacrifices with deep meaning and purpose.

Is the Law Good for Women?

I've written about the importance of approaching Scripture with a Jesus-centered understanding of the Bible and of the need to start from the beginning of Scripture to understand the purpose and heart of God's plan for women. I've covered important stories about women like Ruth, Rahab, and Esther and the meaning to be drawn from them. But even though the stories of those women are far from rosy, other biblical stories of women are far harsher. And it's in those stories we find much of the struggle to believe that the Bible is good for women.* Rachel Held Evans wrote,

> Those who seek to glorify biblical womanhood have
> forgotten the dark stories. They have forgotten that the
> concubine of Bethlehem, the raped princess of David's
> house, the daughter of Jephthah, and the countless
> unnamed women who lived and died between the lines

---

* This chapter discusses sexual assault in Scripture. Please know that, despite my efforts to guard against insensitive or harmful words, there are likely trigger phrases and scenarios in this chapter. If you are a survivor of sexual abuse or assault, I hope you will feel free to skip this chapter. If you choose to read it, know that God sees your wounds and cares deeply for your healing.

of Scripture exploited, neglected, ravaged, and crushed at the hand of patriarchy are as much a part of our shared narrative as Deborah, Esther, Rebekah, and Ruth.[1]

The criticism in this quote is legitimate. We can't have an honest conversation about God's vision for women by noting only the blessings on the honored women in Scripture, the ones with relatively good earthly outcomes. But with an eternal, redemptive backdrop, we start to see an arc of story in Scripture that gives meaning both to troubling passages regarding women as well as the ones with which we traditionally prefer to identify.

Remember from chapter 1 that we are putting off the separate-file-folder approach to the stories of the Bible. In that paradigm, individual stories are limited in value to whatever moral lesson they teach. The result of that approach is that we have no clear category in which to put confusing or hard stories that don't seem to contribute a distinct lesson. In contrast, a Jesus-centered understanding of Scripture helps us engage with such hard stories, because that gospel understanding gives us hope for their purposes in God's larger plan.

DINAH

Genesis has several hard stories about women. Hagar's abuse in Abraham's household in Genesis 16 and 21 gives me pause. But her persecution came primarily through another woman, Sarah. In terms of the struggle between the genders (see Genesis 3), I am particularly struck by the story of Dinah in Genesis 34. Although it was Sarah, Hagar's mistress, who persecuted Hagar, Dinah's life was violently affected by the various men in her life. She was impacted not just by the man who violated her but also by the men who bore retribution against him. Dinah's story is a case study in the issue of oppression between the sexes in God's fallen world.

> Dinah the daughter of Leah, whom she had borne to Jacob, went out to see the women of the land. And when Shechem the son of Hamor the Hivite, the prince of the land, saw her, he seized her and lay with her and humiliated her. And his soul was drawn to Dinah the daughter of Jacob. He loved the young woman and spoke tenderly to her. So Shechem spoke to his father Hamor, saying, "Get me this girl for my wife." (verses 1–4)

Shechem and Hamor then approached Jacob and his sons and offered to pay whatever price they asked for Dinah's hand in marriage. But Dinah's brothers lied to Shechem, promising her hand if Shechem and his men would be circumcised. While the men were sore after being circumcised, Simeon and Levi entered the city and killed all the males. They took their women and children captive and plundered their houses and wealth.

> Then Jacob said to Simeon and Levi, "You have brought trouble on me by making me stink to the inhabitants of the land, the Canaanites and the Perizzites. My numbers are few, and if they gather themselves against me and attack me, I shall be destroyed, both I and my household."

But they said, "Should he treat our sister like a prostitute?"
(verses 30–31)

With her brothers' question, Dinah's story ended. She'd been violated and marginalized. Her brothers killed all the men associated with her abuser, they captured their women and children, and nothing is heard of Dinah again. If the Bible ended here, how could it possibly be good for women?

There is value in sitting in the discomfort of Scripture's silence at this point. If you have a strong negative emotional response to the lack of redemption or resolution to her story, consider why. Because we are God's image bearers, there is something written on our hearts that rightfully chafes at the unresolved, unredeemed sin against Dinah.

But four hundred years later, God gave to Moses a chapter in the Law that addressed Dinah's situation. Her story wasn't lost. It mattered to God, as He gave instructions on the protection for a woman who found herself in Dinah's situation.

The problem is that Deuteronomy 22, where these laws are given, also feels harsh toward women. How can these laws be part of a Bible that is good for women? Let's consider that.

FASCINATING AND DIFFICULT

Deuteronomy 22 is fascinating in its variety of instructions. It starts with basic laws that reflect common decency (though not so common in that day, apparently): be a good neighbor and brother, and help others when they need it even if you don't personally benefit. The chapter then delves into some strange laws, such as forbidding men and women to wear the other gender's clothing and how to handle a bird's nest found on the ground. There are health and human safety laws similar to those of our present-day OSHA (Occupational Safety and Health Administration), such as requiring a guardrail around the roofs of houses to prevent people from falling from them. There are instructions to not make clothing that mixes wool and linen. This law made no sense to me until I mixed up woolen and synthetic yarn in a blanket I made for my son. At each washing, the wool shrank, while the other yarn kept its shape. In a few months, the blanket was warped and practically unusable. I'm not sure how much that is tied to God's purpose in that particular law, but I now see the practical benefit of it for people with few resources, who needed garments to last a long time.

After those instructions, the chapter gets into sexual ethics, including laws to restrain a culture that often oppressed women. The first set of laws called the people to discipline a man who falsely accuses his wife of not being a virgin in an attempt to annul the marriage. The Law gives elaborate instructions to prove her virginity and punish the man for his manipulation. Although our Western feminist culture would cry out against the emphasis on *her* virginity, God's Law instead allows for the emphasis and protects her from the shame of a false accusation.

Conservative culture remains focused on female chastity in a way that often lacks an understanding of the point of God's laws in Deuteronomy 22. This hyperfocus projects a lesser status onto women who have lost their virginity prior to Christian marriage, even if it was lost against their will, while men often get a free pass. If you will stick with me through this and the next chapter, we will see that a Jesus-centered understanding of the law frees us from shame and condemnation over our sexual histories.

One thing becomes increasingly clear as Deuteronomy 22 progresses: God hates, and I mean *hates,* sexual unfaithfulness. "If the thing is true, that evidence of virginity was not found in the young woman, then they shall bring out the young woman to the door of her father's house, and the men of her city shall stone her to death with stones, because she has done an outrageous thing in Israel by whoring in her father's house" (verses 20–21).

This is hard to read, particularly if you hold a Western feminist cultural understanding of sex. First, note that God does not say that the woman's virginity matters and the man's does not. The simple fact is there was no way to confirm physically whether the man was a virgin. Also, it does not appear that women in that culture were trying to dishonor their spouses to get out of their marriage vows the way some men were. In other laws in the Old Testament, punishment was equally pronounced among men and women committing sexual sins. Over time, cultures warped toward inconsistently prizing female virginity over male, but that is the result of a perverted view of gender after the Fall, not the result of instructions in the Bible.

Nevertheless, it is tempting from our modern cultural views of sex to write off Deuteronomy 22 as archaic and barbaric. But there is value to this chapter of Scripture well beyond prizing virginity, and it is worthwhile to wrestle with this text until we understand it.

What if we value this chapter for its context within the larger story of Scripture? What if we approach it as Jesus did? A Jesus-centered understanding of Scripture gives us the ability to see what this particular law was intended to teach us about God and then to see Jesus as the fulfillment of it. Jesus fulfills both the righteousness that the law called us to and the punishment that it proclaimed over those who violated it. He paid the penalty of our debt and also placed on us His robe of righteousness, counting us as if we had obeyed the Law perfectly (see 2 Corinthians 5:21). This gives us freedom to approach these laws without fear. Whatever the Law projects onto us, Jesus erases it and projects a better image through faith in Him.

THE IMAGE OF GOD AND THE LAW

Before we can get to how Jesus fulfilled the Law, we need to first understand what it is teaching us about God. Through the Old Testament Law, God commanded of His image bearers the things He valued in Himself. How should people who are set apart to reflect a holy God view sex? In Deuteronomy 22, God set up the sexual ethic He valued, which was total fidelity between partners. It wasn't partial fidelity. It was not generally valuing monogamy. If you read through the whole of the chapter, you see that God values *complete* faithfulness from beginning to end in marriage. Both adultery involving a married man or woman and fornication between two who were unmarried and not betrothed to another were punishable by death.

Unlike our modern Western culture, in which the breaking

of engagement and marriage vows has little stigma attached, betrothal between a man and a woman in ancient Israel reflected a
deep commitment, not just between individuals but also between
their families. In their harsh world, allies who could be trusted as
family were crucial to flourishing life. The breaking of vows between families had horrible consequences. This remains true in
many cultures today. Fidelity in family relationships was the foundation on which that society rose or fell.

But even more than societal stability, God was serious about
His children's fidelity to each other because He is serious about
His fidelity to them.

THE FIDELITY OF GOD

Scripture gives numerous pictures of God's fidelity. One of the
most powerful is found in the book of Hosea. As God said to His
prophet in 2:19–20, "I will betroth you to me forever. I will betroth you to me in righteousness and in justice, in steadfast love
and in mercy. I will betroth you to me in faithfulness. And you
shall know the LORD."

Betrothal was supposed to mean something serious to God's
children because His betrothal to us means something serious to
God. God is a loyal, covenant-keeping God. He is faithful to His
people He created in His likeness, and He instructs them to be
faithful to their commitments as well.

God spoke words in Hosea 2 of His steadfast love and mercy
in the context of His instructions to Hosea to pursue his adulterous bride, not with the intent to stone her to death according to

the Law but rather to return her to her honored position in Ho-sea's home. By using Hosea to understand Deuteronomy 22, we see that God's rigid call to fidelity in marriage in the law of Deuteronomy reflects the best of His character and the most beautiful of His virtues. It reflects the grace of His commitment to us and our security in Him. Though there are consequences to our sin, despite it all, He will not quit on us! Paul reminds us of this in 2 Timothy 2:13: "If we are faithless, he remains faith-ful—for he cannot deny himself."

But how do God's faithfulness and grace, the pursuit of an adulterous bride, and the Law connect to the story arc of Dinah? How is her tragic story redeemed and a demonstration of how the Bible is good for women? Digging deeper into the laws in Deuter-onomy 22 will guide us on this journey.

CULTURAL CONCERNS

First we need to face the cultural concerns we bring to the table because of advances in personal rights that the original audience of Deuteronomy 22 would not have known. When I approach a chapter like Deuteronomy 22 from my understanding of women's rights, these laws on immorality and fidelity feel very uncomfort-able. It seems easier to write off the Law as archaic than to value its reflection of God and recognize the ways I might violate its ethic of faithfulness. I believe there are two values from my par-ticular Western cultural upbringing—rugged individualism and self-determination—that contribute to this reaction.

These are important American values, and during my years

living in the Pacific Northwest, I recognized individualism and self-determination as strongly held ideals, particularly in that rough, remote part of the United States. Anecdotal evidence suggests that faith in the God of the Bible takes a hit in cultures where the individual is elevated above the group.[2] This is likely due, at least in part, to the fact that the Old Testament sets up a God-ordained cultural system that values the whole, that values communal good. It's not that God's system doesn't value the individual, but it sets up a philosophy in which the individual prospers when the group prospers.

In the New Testament as well, individual believers are assimilated into a corporate structure, the body of Christ. The Bible gives instruction to value each other's role in the whole. The eye cannot say to the hand that it has no need for the other, according to 1 Corinthians 12. If one part suffers, the whole suffers, and when the whole flourishes, it means the individual parts are flourishing as well.

One specific cultural issue of self-determination that plays into the instructions of Deuteronomy 22 is our approach to arranged marriages. From my Western vantage point, it's hard to conceive of entering a long-term, committed relationship with someone when I had little vote. Yet cultures that value the flourishing of the corporate whole over rugged individualism and self-determination approach arranged marriages differently, even today. I suspected this was true before doing any research, but I had to talk directly to those in such cultures to understand it. Through conversations with those who had firsthand experience, I realized that what I accepted as normative was a Western approach to marriage. Many other cultures believe that the family collective is wiser than the individual on such an important decision.

A friend told me how her parents' marriage was arranged. Her grandparents selected three prospective brides for her father based on many different factors, not just attraction or chemistry. Although chemistry would have been a bonus, the families looked more for alignment of values that would contribute to long-term harmony. Her parents learned attraction through the harmony of their aligned lives rather than vice versa. As this friend recounted stories of various family members' arranged marriages with both good outcomes and bad, I came to understand that abuse of women is not inherent in arranged marriages any more than it is in marriages of individual choice. When I realized I was projecting my Western values onto a text written to people living in ancient Middle Eastern cultures, it enabled me to better understand what God communicates of Himself in Deuteronomy 22.

PROTECTIONS IN THE LAW FROM ABUSE

While arranged marriage did not create abuse, neither did it protect from abuse. In Deuteronomy 22, Scripture recognizes and gives instruction about two potentially abusive situations. I've already written about one: the protection from discrediting wives with unjust accusations about their virginity at marriage. But Deuteronomy 22 also addresses Dinah's situation in Genesis 34. This is the next point in the arc of Dinah's story, though it came centuries after her life.

The Law states, "If a man meets a virgin who is not betrothed, and seizes her and lies with her, and they are found,
then the man who lay with her shall give to the father of the
young woman fifty shekels of silver, and she shall be his wife,
because he has violated her. He may not divorce her all his days"
(Deuteronomy 22:28–29).

Rapists were commanded to marry their victims. We need to
acknowledge that this is a tough piece of Scripture to wrestle
with—one that causes many to shut their Bibles and pronounce
that the Bible is without question bad for women. This instruction feels highly offensive as our society grows in its understanding of consent, the trauma of rape, and the culpability of a man
who commits such an act.

Note that this command in Deuteronomy 22 is not to a
woman to marry her rapist; it's a command to a rapist to marry
the woman he wronged. That difference is noteworthy for yet another troubling reason: a woman had few choices and rights in
that ancient culture. Whether he married her or not, apart from
the Law, she was powerless to affect the outcome either way.

It's important to recognize that when God gave the Law, civilization was not very civilized. A common practice outside the
Law for a woman who was raped was that her family killed her
because of the resulting shame (a practice still occurring in some
cultures today).[3] Mankind was bent far away from basic human
dignity at this early point in the unfurling story of God's redemption of His people, some fourteen hundred years before the birth
of Jesus. At this point in the story of Scripture, a major theme is
the way mankind had fallen short of the glory for which it was

created. Humankind had been warped away from reflecting God's image in themselves or recognizing it in others. People primarily lived by survival of the fittest, where the weak were despised or used for personal gain, not cherished as image bearers of God worthy of respect. If a rape survivor's family did not kill her, she was left to live in shame with no options for a future life with a family. She likely could support herself only through prostitution. Apart from the Law, not only had she been abused, but she was a prime target for future abuse.

In cultures throughout the world, including my own American one, I see many men today who still view sexual conquest as a game with no consequences. Their hearts are hardened to the harm caused to the ones they violate. Though it might not initially appear this way, the law in Deuteronomy actually gave the survivor of rape a path to a respectable life in her culture as well as protection from future exploitation. This law held the man responsible for the consequences he created through his sin against the woman. He had to pay her father a price worthy of the woman he violated, and he could never divorce her. The law required him to remove the victim's shame and restore her to a position of dignity in her community. From this perspective, this law is meaningful for a woman so violated in a culture that apart from God's laws had *no* safeguards. In this chapter of Deuteronomy, we see that Dinah's story *did* matter to God and that the violation she endured was offensive to God long after her death. The law of Deuteronomy 22 presented the violated with a path to dignity. The abuser was made to value what he took without right.

I am thankful to live in a culture today that doesn't cast upon a woman (at least not as much) the same shame and condemnation that was the norm in ancient times and is still the norm in parts of the world today. But in a culture that did, God pressed upon His people a way forward that not only gave the victim marriage but also required a sizable payment for the *privilege* of marrying her. God's plan did not just remove her shame but also provided for her security by requiring a monetary commitment to her and her family.

Reclothing the Abused

A few years ago my former church scheduled a retreat for survivors of sexual sin. Organizers wanted to demonstrate to attendees a concept called reclothing a survivor of sexual abuse. A woman gave a raw testimony of her past sexual abuse. Afterward, a pastor stood by her and spoke of both her preciousness to God and his respect for her in our congregation. He acknowledged her vulnerability from both the pain of her sexual history and exposing it to those at the retreat. He spoke words to and over her, reminding her of her dignity as God's daughter. What this pastor did was a beautiful example of reclothing with honor and value someone who had endured much evil.

Deuteronomy 22 shows us a woman who had been stripped physically and emotionally. God commanded His children to reclothe her—to put back on her the status and respect that her abuser stole and to provide for her physically so she would no longer be vulnerable. Mike Wilkerson, author of *Redemption,* calls this *gracing,* which he defines as extending God's one-way, steadfast love that accepts and blesses others, especially in times of need and defenselessness. The psalmist wrote that God "will cover you with his feathers, and under his wings you will find refuge" (Psalm 91:4, NIV). God covers us in our vulnerability and called His children in Deuteronomy 22 to do the same to others.

Even in understanding how these laws elevated a woman in that ancient cultural context, we still have real concerns. We might ask why the Israelites didn't put the rapist in jail and remove the woman's shame in other ways. But there were no jails in those days. The punitive options in the Law generally required a violator to repair what he had harmed or be stoned. If the people stoned him, he would certainly be punished, but the woman would still be left without a path to respectability. In the event that the woman was betrothed and had another man who would provide for her, the one who violated her was put to death according to the Law (see Deuteronomy 22:25).

Perhaps our real concern is why our good God didn't move these people from their cultural understanding to ours more quickly than He did. This is just one of many situations in Scripture of which we could ask that. Why did God write a story that lasted at least six thousand years? Why did He wait four hundred years between Dinah's rape and giving the laws that addressed it? But we ask questions like these as earthbound creatures, at least in our perception of reality. God is eternal, and He calls us to live in light of eternity as well. God's sense of time is not the same as ours. If a thousand years is as one day to Him, then the movement from those laws to today has not been slow at all from His kingdom-building perspective (see 2 Peter 3:8).

JESUS AND THE LAW

In our examination of Dinah's account, even if we value the removal of shame from the victim that Deuteronomy 22 instructs, the arc of her story is not yet complete. Although the Law addressed Dinah's situation, it did not make men righteous or end all abuse. Greater insight comes if we fast-forward from Deuteronomy to the moment when the woman caught in adultery was thrown at Jesus's feet just before men planned to stone her.*

> The scribes and the Pharisees brought a woman who had been caught in adultery, and placing her in the midst they said to him, "Teacher, this woman has been caught in the act of adultery. Now in the Law Moses commanded us to stone such women. So what do you say?" This they said to test him, that they might have some charge to bring against him. Jesus bent down and wrote with his finger on the ground. And as they continued to ask him, he stood up and said to them, "Let him who is without sin among you be the first to throw a stone at her." And once more he bent down and wrote on the ground. But when they heard it, they went away one by one, beginning with the older ones, and Jesus was left alone with the woman

---

* Though many accept this story of the woman caught in adultery as part of the canon of Scripture, debate on its authenticity has focused on the fact that it is missing from the earliest manuscripts of John's gospel. I continue to treat it as part of the canon of Scripture; regardless, its principles are reinforced in other passages not in question, such as Luke 7's account of Jesus and the sinful woman.

standing before him. Jesus stood up and said to her,
"Woman, where are they? Has no one condemned you?"
She said, "No one, Lord." And Jesus said, "Neither do I
condemn you; go, and from now on sin no more." (John
8:3–11)

In this moment, we see that whatever protection Deuteronomy 22 was supposed to provide women, it had failed. If her
partner was married, it failed the wife of the man with whom
she was caught as well as the adulterous woman herself, neither
keeping her from sin that harmed another family nor equitably
punishing her male partner in the sin. Despite the law's description of equal punishment in the case of adultery, the man's status in the community was likely valued above hers. Although
Jewish leaders sought to extract the letter of the law in punishment from the woman, the man was apparently left to go on
without consequences.

In Galatians 3:19–26, the apostle Paul is up-front about the
inadequacies of the Law that are demonstrated in John 8. All the
Law managed to do, at its very best, was restrain sin in a limited
capacity. The Law teaches us what God values, but it doesn't effec-
tively change us so that we consistently honor those values. Modern, Western laws might restrain better, but they don't work
perfectly either. In talking with friends abused in similar ways to
Dinah, I found that many still feel underserved by the laws that
should have protected them from the sin committed against them.
And many also feel that the laws should have more adequately punished the ones who abused them.

Why then the law? It was added because of transgressions, until the offspring should come to whom the promise had been made. . . .

Now before faith came, we were held captive under the law, imprisoned until the coming faith would be revealed. So then, the law was our guardian until Christ came, in order that we might be justified by faith. But now that faith has come, we are no longer under a guardian, for in Christ Jesus you are all sons of God, through faith. (Galatians 3:19, 23–26)

Paul teaches here in Galatians 3 that the Old Testament Law primarily made us more aware of our sin. The Law was a guardian, Paul says, an imperfect tutor waiting for Jesus to come. In the interaction between Jesus and the woman caught violating the adultery laws of Deuteronomy 22, we get a glimpse of what Paul is teaching.

More than simply seeing the inadequacy of the Law to restrain sin, I am moved by Jesus's words as I watch the only One to ever fully keep the Law offer grace to this one who had clearly broken it. Jesus didn't offer this grace in a way that undermined the value of God's Law on fidelity in marriage. He said to her, "Go, and from now on sin no more" (John 8:11). This is consistent with His message in the Gospels. He forgave sins, but in so doing He reinforced the righteousness such sins affronted. "Sin no more," He told the man healed at the pool of Bethesda in John 5. "Your sins are forgiven," He told both the paralytic before He healed him in Mark 2 and the shamed woman who washed His feet with her hair in Luke 7.

Pastor and professor Zack Eswine says, "Both the Devil and God talk about sin. But their impact differs dramatically."[4] Concerning the woman in John 8, both Jesus and the Pharisees spoke of her violation of the Law. But while one group sought to kill her, Jesus offered something radically different. After He noted that this woman's accusers no longer stood to condemn her, Jesus said, "Neither do I condemn you" (verse 11). It isn't just the Pharisees' condemnation that Jesus thwarted; it was God's very own condemnation—the foundation of the Law that resulted in her being thrown at Jesus's feet—that Jesus pronounced satisfied! When Jesus announced, "Neither do I condemn you," God Himself was releasing her, in light of Jesus's coming death, from the weight of guilt that Deuteronomy 22 pronounced over her.

Paul writes in Romans 8:1, "There is . . . no condemnation for those who are in Christ Jesus." This is either beautiful to you or extremely frustrating. It may make you tear up with joy, or it may cause you deep anger. What makes the difference in our reactions is how we view our own sinfulness. Those who get angry appreciate a Jesus who doesn't condemn, but they don't care for one who forgives sins. We can remove condemnation without acknowledging guilt: "I don't condemn you, because what you did wasn't worthy of condemnation." Most of us appreciate a removal of condemnation that validates the actions that led to the condemnation in the first place. In contrast, Jesus freed the adulterous woman from condemnation without undermining God's strong feelings on the scourge of adultery. Jesus forgives sins, and inherent in both the words *forgiveness* and *sin* is that we were wrong and deserved condemnation. Jesus's phrasing humbles us and calls us to self-inspection. Condemnation is removed, but not because this woman committed no actions worthy of condemnation.

Our Very Good God

We began this chapter by looking at the story of Dinah. Through the laws given in Deuteronomy 22, we see that her violation mattered to God. God instructed His people to remove the shame from His image bearers who were being treated sexually as less than human. But Deuteronomy 22 also links Dinah's story to the woman of John 8 who was not a victim but a perpetrator. The woman of John 8 had committed adultery, either violating her own vows or participating in a husband's violation of his. Dinah was innocent in her situation; the woman from John 8 was a willing participant in hers. What we see in the Gospels is that Jesus doesn't remove just the shame of the victim but also the shame of the perpetrator.* Women, we see, can be both victimized and victimizer, abused and abuser. Jesus offers something to both.

I love the God who removes the shame from those who have

---

* The issue of mercy for an abuser can trigger strong emotions in the one abused. If that is your situation, I encourage you to know that the mercy Jesus offered in John 8 was not to a rapist but to a woman caught in adultery. The juxtaposition between Dinah and this woman is not between a rape survivor and her rapist but between one innocent in a crime against her and one willingly breaking the Law herself. We know that God offers mercy to even the murderer, and He offers it to the rapist as well. But if you are not yet ready to consider that gospel implication for the one who harmed you, just consider it today in this woman's situation and meditate on Jesus's mercy to her. The day will likely come when you are ready for other gospel implications, but it is okay if today is not that day.

been sinned against. But I am thrown to my knees with arms raised in praise for the grace of Jesus that also removes the shame of sin for the repentant perpetrator. There is no condemnation for the sins against us, though many cultures still project shame on victims of such sin. But there is also no condemnation for the sins we have committed. Yet, through it all, Jesus doesn't normalize sin. Jesus directs us still to sin no more. His bloody crucifixion shows the heaviness of the sins you and I have committed against God and that others have committed against us.

Your sins are forgiven, Jesus says. Go, and sin no more. He alone is the One that equips you and me to reclaim God's image in us and live in light of that dignity.

What Instructions Are for Today?

As we work through the question of the title of this book, we have looked at the creation, fall, and redemption arc of story in the Bible to understand the meaning it gives the lives of women in the Old Testament. We have focused on a long view of the story of Scripture and God's eternal purposes to give meaning to the suffering and exaltation of various women in its pages. But many controversial passages about women remain, particularly in the New Testament, that we have not addressed. We have examined how the arc of story informs shorter stories within the big story. We also need to understand how this arc of story informs the instructions to obey and doctrines to internalize given in Scripture. When someone questions if the Bible is good for women, that person is often asking if its *instructions* are good for women and if there is any value in obeying them in the twenty-first century.

Once someone understands how all of Scripture ultimately points to Jesus, it is helpful to learn how to read different parts of Scripture. Otherwise we have no frame of reference for knowing what commands God expects us to still follow. And even if we understand which passages are for today, many of us have had commands and instructions used against us in careless ways. Therefore, we need to understand as well how to approach commands for today from a position of grace so we won't be afraid to apply them. We have a lot to accomplish in this chapter!

UNIVERSAL VERSUS TEMPORARY COMMANDS

At times, God wrote out His revelation of Himself to us in the form of stories. Sometimes He used clear commands and instructions. Within even those clear commands and instructions, God gave universal truths for all cultures and all times—"You shall not murder" (Exodus 20:13)—along with instructions that played a specific role for a finite period of time: "The pig, because it parts the hoof but does not chew the cud, is unclean for you. Their flesh you shall not eat, and their carcasses you shall not touch" (Deuteronomy 14:8).

It's fairly easy to understand why Christians are no longer forbidden to eat pork but are still required to preserve life. The Bible gives a long description in Acts 10 of how God communicated to His children that the dietary laws of the Old Testament were no longer binding while reaffirming the Ten Commandments throughout the New Testament. The difference between committing murder and eating pork makes sense to most of us. But the same principles of reading the Bible that help us understand those passages also help us grasp other passages not as easily distinguished from each other. In this particular case, the Bible itself reveals to us that the dietary laws are fulfilled. How does Scripture reveal what other parts of it, particularly laws and instructions, were for a particular time, and what parts transcend time or culture?

To understand what part of Scripture applies to us today, we first need to examine the difference between *prescriptive* and *descriptive* texts. Then we will distinguish between three types of prescriptive Scriptural passages—Old Testament Law, proverbs, and New Testament instructions—to understand how we should apply them to our lives. Finally, in chapter 8, we will look at various hard passages concerning women in the New Testament and examine their role in the larger narrative of Jesus.

PRESCRIPTION VERSUS DESCRIPTION

My biggest frustration with those who claim that the Bible is bad for women is that they fail to distinguish between texts that prescribe what to do (such as "Don't have sex with someone else's husband") and what a character in Scripture did or experienced (such as the rape of Dinah). One is what Scripture says to do, and the other is how Scripture describes what happened. One is prescriptive, the other descriptive.

> Prescriptive: "giving exact rules, directions, or instructions about how you should do something."[1]

> Descriptive: "relating to or based upon description or classification rather than explanation or prescription."[2]

Prescriptive texts in the Bible direct us to do something. Descriptive texts in the Bible give an account of something that happened without necessarily ascribing to it positive or negative value. If we aren't careful to understand the difference between these two categories, our attempts to understand what does and does not apply to us today can quickly become muddled.

Consider the book of Judges, which has several troubling stories about women, particularly two major ones. The first involved Jephthah's daughter, whom it seems was sacrificed after her father made a misguided vow to God (see Judges 11), and the second was an account of a Levite cutting up his concubine after sending her to be raped and abused by strangers in the city (see Judges 19).[3] These are horrible accounts of life in Israel during that time. Judges 19 opens with the words, "In those days Israel had no king" (NIV). What follows is a description of life in that setting. The children of God had no king, and the very last words of the book tell us the result of this lack: *Everyone did what was right in his own eyes* (21:25).

Judges is descriptive. Rather than prescribing what we should do today, Judges instead tells the history of God's children who looked to themselves rather than God's instructions to decide what they should or should not do. Judges doesn't reflect a God who is bad for women or a Bible that is bad for women, but it does tell us of a fallen world that, apart from God and obedience to Scripture, often harmed and abused women.

Judges describes, in particular, the weaknesses of both the system of judges and the law previously given to Moses. It points to Israel's need for a king, but later we see that the earthly kings were no better than the judges, and with few exceptions, everyone continued to do what was right in their own eyes. Instead, they needed a perfect King who would give the perfect standard of righteousness and equip them to keep it. Our Jesus-centered understanding of Scripture enables us to see Judges for what it is: an account of people with warped senses of right and wrong who often made horrible choices. They were the essence of fallen humanity, doing right in their own eyes without examining themselves in light of the Creator they were called to image or His instructions for them. We recognize now that they needed King Jesus as both Savior and example.

We can and should mourn the plight of the women abused in Judges. This does not undermine the truth or goodness of Scripture. We must also clearly recognize the fallen humanity their stories reflect. If we understand the basic difference in prescriptive and descriptive passages, we have the first key to understanding troublesome passages about women in the Bible.

DISCERNING BETWEEN PRESCRIPTIVE TEXTS

While distinguishing between descriptive and prescriptive texts in Scripture is fairly easy, we are still left with questions about understanding prescriptive passages. How do we interact with Scripture that tells us what to do and clearly calls us to obey it? Prescriptive passages include Wisdom Literature, Old Testament Law, and New Testament instructions. How is reading the Wisdom Literature different from reading the Law? How is the Law read in light of the New Testament? How is the rest of the New Testament to be understood with respect to the Gospels? The answers to these questions help us understand troubling passages concerning women.

We discussed how to read the Law in chapter 6 and the difference between law and proverbs in chapter 3. We know from Jesus's words in Matthew 5:17 that He didn't come to undermine the Old Testament Law but rather to fulfill it. In Galatians 3, the apostle Paul gives us even more commentary on what this means. The Law taught us about our need for Jesus because of both our sinfulness as the Law revealed the holiness of God and our inability to keep the Law no matter how much we might value it. It was a "tutor," Paul says, but we no longer need this tutor (see verses 24–25, NASB). Through Christ we are equipped to understand the character of our God that the Law was to teach us, and through Christ we are able to enjoy peace with Him despite our failures. The Law is fulfilled, and its instructions are no longer binding. Yet we can still value the Law for what it teaches us of image bearing, even though we are free from being judged by it.

We have talked about image bearing in the Law's instructions on faithfulness in marriage. But the Law also included a lot of practical help that brought civilization to a people who were not very civilized on their own. These men and women had no police, no courts, no OSHA, no medical establishment, and so forth. God had compassion on His children despite their disobedience and did not leave them to figure out everything on their own, the hard way.

In that light, consider Leviticus 15's instructions for women who are on their menstrual cycle. This hearkens back to our discussion of Nepali daughters from the opening of this book. If you read the entire chapter, you will see that the first half of Leviticus 15 discusses similar requirements for men with bodily fluid discharge. Critics of the Bible often indicate that the Law was biased against women on this issue and declared them unclean simply because they were having their periods. But if you approach Scripture without a predisposition to be suspicious, a different image emerges. This is a passage about sanitation regardless of gender.

Frankly, I'm quite thankful for the sanitary advances we've made for both men and women discharging bodily fluid (which is a weird way to say it, but that's how Leviticus 15 refers to it). The children of God at this time didn't have latex gloves or those protective pads that hospitals and nursing homes use to cover beds and chairs. They certainly didn't have maxi pads, tampons, or anything remotely equivalent. Plus, they didn't live in homes with secure doorways to protect them from animals following the scent of blood. It was in everyone's best interest to have clear guidelines surrounding what a woman could and could not do during her cycle so that the remainder of the month was not full of diseases and consequences if blood or other types of discharges were not wisely handled. And remember, Leviticus 15 includes similar instructions for men.

Much of the Law was simply helpful instruction passed down from a Father to His children living in a fallen world. Instead of His children having to learn everything the hard way, from the problems of mixing fabrics in a garment to the need for banisters around one's rooftop, from the gastric issues caused by eating bottom-dwelling shellfish to the dangers caused by infectious diseases, God taught His children much about how life worked through His Law to them. We know that these laws were fulfilled in Christ and we are no longer under them, yet we should recognize the wisdom of God they represented to a people who lacked the medical and sanitary knowledge we have today.

PRESCRIPTIVE PASSAGES REVEAL GOD'S CHARACTER

The Law also served to show civilization what God values (and what we, in turn, should also value). We care about such things as the dignity of human life, care of the poor, fidelity in marriage, fairness in business dealings, and social justice because God first showed us through the Law that He cared about such things. When survival of the fittest was the rule of the day, God spoke strong words to His children of His value system, which included the care of the poor and the immigrant, the widow and the orphan. It gave a way for one to repay a debt and protection to keep the rich from exploiting those without. Today we call it Judeo-Christian ethics. At the root level, the Creator gave the Law to His creatures who, after the Fall, were bent far away from the sense of how humanity should work that would have flowed from an unspoiled Eden.

Not only did the Law bring civilization to uncivilized people, it also showed from different angles both their need for an ultimate Savior and what He would look like when He came. The Law gave extensive instructions on the need to sacrifice an animal for the sins of the people. It taught God's children that they needed a mediator between them and God—that there was a great and holy God whose presence they could not enter in their current state. Instructions for the high priest and the Holy of Holies were somber reminders of the distance between humans and their Father in heaven because of their sins. Instructions pertaining to the lamb without blemish prepared their hearts to receive Jesus when He came (see John 1:29), and their understanding of the Holy of Holies through the Law enabled them to recognize the great importance of the tearing of the veil in the temple when Jesus breathed His last breath (see Matthew 27:51).

How, then, should we receive the various instructions—prescriptive passages—in Scripture? We start in Genesis 1 and 2, where God states in perfection that every woman is an image bearer of God, reflecting especially His strong help and advocacy for His children. From there, I recommend studying Ephesians, where Paul lays out our spiritual inheritance via the gospel as the key to once again being the followers of God He created us to be. In between, the Old Testament Law pointed toward Christ and was fulfilled in Him. Proverbs gives insight, wisdom, and understanding (not law), which is best received under the conviction of the Holy Spirit, who helps us apply it in wise ways to our own lives. The New Testament explicitly reaffirms the summary moral code of the Ten Commandments. Jesus even intensified it in His Sermon on the Mount. This is why New Testament Christians not only speak out against murder but also believe that lashing out in anger is a sin (see Matthew 5:21–22). Jesus boiled down the Law for us so we could continue living in what the Law conveyed to us about God's character and His desires for His children. The essence of the Old Testament Law, Jesus says, is summed up in the Golden Rule and Greatest Commandment:

> Whatever you wish that others would do to you, do also to them, for this is the Law and the Prophets. (Matthew 7:12)

> "Teacher, which is the great commandment in the Law?" And he said to him, "You shall love the Lord your God with all your heart and with all your soul and with all your mind. This is the great and first commandment. And a second is like it: You shall love your neighbor as yourself. On these two commandments depend all the Law and the Prophets." (Matthew 22:36–40)

As we move from the Gospels into the rest of the New Testament, we find many instructions in the epistles of the apostle Paul, Peter, and others. These epistles flesh out what the love of the Greatest Commandment and the care for others of the Golden Rule look like in the New Covenant, and we can trust those instructions even as we wrestle with the Holy Spirit to understand and apply them.

This seems to be where most women struggle with Scripture: the New Testament instructions. The Old Testament Law was an arrow shot from Moses that arched over the people of God until it landed at Jesus's feet in the Gospels. The New Testament instructions function the same way, mirroring many of the Old

Testament laws but with a clear emphasis on the Greatest Command to love God and our neighbor. New Testament instructions put away the types of laws that pointed to the death and resurrection of Jesus, but they still include much to guide us on bearing the image of our Father in heaven as Jesus modeled Him on earth. Most important, the arrow of the New Testament started before our lives, but its landing point is the marriage supper of the Lamb in Revelation.

These New Testament instructions still arch over us to guide us in righteousness today. In that light, there is much to work through in the New Testament concerning the question of the title of this book. But what if we don't feel safe engaging these instructions and commands?

WHEN PRESCRIPTIVE PASSAGES ARE MISHANDLED

I have a history of both prescriptive and descriptive passages used arbitrarily against me in ways that made me nervous about approaching Scripture for a while. You might have as well. I was raised in fundamentalist Christian churches with long lists of rights, wrongs, dos, and don'ts from the Bible that were confusing and often contradictory. Preachers applied the Bible haphazardly and seemed to emphasize the parts of the Bible that best suited their personal agendas. I remember being taught, for instance, that women should not wear pants because, according to Deuteronomy 22:5, women were not supposed to wear "that which pertaineth unto a man" (KJV). Yet I noted the inconsistent way

Scripture was used, for these same preachers did not have a problem with church members wearing cotton/polyester blend clothing despite similar warnings against mixed fabrics just six verses later in the same chapter of the Law. Why was I supposed to not wear clothing that a man wore but it wasn't a problem if my dress was a blend of fabrics?

On top of the random and inconsistent use of Scripture, youth-group leaders regularly taught prohibitions "from the Bible" that I figured out later weren't actually in the Bible at all. It wasn't enough to obey God's explicit instructions in the Bible. Leaders would regularly project onto kids their personal convictions based on general Bible principles. They were so afraid the kids would violate black-and-white commands that they turned the gray areas around such commands into black as well. I was again confused at how I could know from Scripture what God did and did not expect of me to obey as a twenty-first-century Christian. So I definitely had baggage as I approached Scripture in adulthood.

I came to a deeper understanding of God's grace through Christ by way of my freshman roommate in college, who remains one of my closest friends. With her help, God started tying Scriptures together in my head, and the individual moral lessons of Scripture began to point to Christ rather than to my inadequacies. Learning of God's grace and sovereignty was a balm to my soul, which had been battered by legalistic, extrabiblical teaching (teaching that went well beyond what the Bible actually said) that vexed me again and again. God loved me, and I loved Him. Christianity wasn't about what I could do for God; it was about what He had done for me when I was still far from Him.

For a while, that was enough. I took a break from the theme of preachers from my youth, over-the-top self-examination for whether or not I was obeying the intent of every command of Scripture. I bathed in the teachings of irresistible grace, unearned mercy, and unconditional love for a decade or so. They were like a warm Epsom salt bath for my weary spiritual body. My muscles relaxed. I could breathe again. I didn't have to earn my righteousness to be approved by God. Christ had earned it, and that was enough.

I loved God's grace to me through Christ, but I had to learn again how to love His commands as well. Have you similarly had Scripture used against you? Do you fear considering God's instructions because of that? I have turned a corner of late, and I hope to inspire you to do so as well. I still love the robe of Jesus's righteousness I wear (see Isaiah 61:10), but I've arisen from the warm tub that eased my spiritual wounds. I feel equipped again to note the many other verses in Scripture defining the acts making up the fabric of Jesus's robe of righteousness as opposed to the ones that make up the essence of my guilt: God's fidelity versus my faithlessness. His truth versus my lies. His wisdom versus my foolishness. His peace versus my anger. His love for others versus my love for myself. Jesus's humility versus my stubborn pride. I see too the verses calling me now, in Christ, to be like Him: "It is enough for the disciple to be like his teacher, and the servant like his master" (Matthew 10:25).

If we are in Christ, wearing Jesus's robe of righteousness, we are now equipped to move toward being in reality what God has declared us to be in heaven—completely righteous. He counts us as having already kept all of the relevant Bible instructions, but He also calls us to actively appropriate them in our lives. They bless us.

Of course, we will not immediately obey God perfectly here on earth. We are all sinners declared righteous (called *justification* in theological circles). But after God justifies us through Christ, He begins the process toward true righteousness, called *sanctification*. This is where we become in reality on earth what God has already declared us to be in heaven. This takes a lifetime and isn't finished until we reach heaven, and it is also brought about by God's grace working in us. As Paul asks in Galatians 3:3, "Are you so foolish? Having begun by the Spirit, are you now being perfected by the flesh?" The author of Hebrews quotes Jeremiah, who said that the Law is now written on our hearts (see Hebrews 10:16). What God did externally through His Law in the Old Covenant, He now does internally through the Holy Spirit in the New Covenant.

I like the idea of growing in righteousness by God's grace through the Holy Spirit and not my own fleshly works. And for many of God's commandments through which the Spirit calls and equips me to reflect Him, I have no struggle. Don't kill. Don't lie. Don't rob. Do love. Do seek peace. Do care for the least of these. I value these commands, as do most people I know, regardless of their belief in the God of the Bible. But what about commandments that don't seem to serve the common good in the same way that prohibitions against murder or stealing do? What about something like Paul's instructions in Ephesians 5 regarding

husbands and wives? Or Deuteronomy 22, which includes instructions on fabrics and birds' nests along with its powerful statements on sexual ethics? What is the value of considering such
instructions, laws, and teachings in Scripture if I don't depend on
them for my righteousness before God? And how can I approach
these laws and instructions in a consistent way that honors the
way the Bible talks about itself?

What does it look like to approach morality from a position of grace? How does it look to value all of God's instructions from my secure vantage point, wearing Christ's robe of
righteousness? I would be a poor steward of the gospel if I at-
tempted to write about the biblical instructions we need to keep
today without making sure we are on the same page about how
we can approach them without condemnation in Christ. At
times, I haven't wanted to know what the Bible says to do or not
to do because I didn't want it to be used again as a bludgeon
against me. I stuck my fingers in my ears singing the ABC song
rather than approaching Scripture with an open mind if I
thought what it said might limit me. Can God's perfect love really cast out my fears when I examine Scriptural teachings (see
1 John 4:18)? Security in Him and confidence in His perfect
love for me has empowered me to reengage instructions, laws,
and commandments in Scripture that my fundamentalist upbringing misused against me. Clothed in Christ's righteousness,
I don't feel threatened by reading Scripture's instructions at face
value anymore. I hope you feel this way too as we approach various New Testament instructions in chapter 8.

COLOSSIANS AS A CASE STUDY

Consider the book of Colossians, which I loved for its emphasis on grace as I was leaving fundamentalism. Paul opens it with a long discussion of the wonder of Jesus who "has delivered us from the domain of darkness and transferred us to the kingdom of his beloved Son, in whom we have redemption, the forgiveness of sins" (1:13–14). Paul goes on to say that through Jesus, God has reconciled "to himself all things, whether on earth or in heaven, making peace by the blood of his cross. And you, who once were alienated and hostile in mind, doing evil deeds, he has now reconciled in his body of flesh by his death, in order to present you holy and blameless and above reproach before him" (verses 20–22).

The strife is over. We are reconciled to God! This message of grace and forgiveness flows through Colossians 1. But note that if we keep reading in Colossians, when we get to chapter 3, we see that this reconciliation leads to something else, something that doesn't earn our righteousness (we are already presented as blameless and above reproach wearing Christ's righteousness) but something that helps us live in light of it: "If then you have been raised with Christ, seek the things that are above, where Christ is, seated at the right hand of God. Set your minds on things that are above, not on things that are on earth. For you have died, and your life is hidden with Christ in God" (verses 1–3).

I find Paul's wording in Colossians 3:1 interesting. We have been *raised* with Christ, so we should seek the things that are *above*. I have an image in my head of someone who has moved from a dirty, unfinished basement in a building to the penthouse suite on the top floor but wants to keep taking the elevator down to use the nasty basement restrooms. It isn't that he needs to use the penthouse restrooms or kitchen to keep his residence on the penthouse level, but it doesn't make sense anymore to keep going down when he has access to much better on the upper floor.

We've been raised up out of our dead state in sin. We don't live below ground in a coffin anymore, and we now have access to the air and sun above. That should lead us to think about and pursue the things that are above, informed by Christ's place at the right hand of God.

MORAL ISSUES FROM THE TOP FLOOR

Paul then applies this to moral issues in the next verses in Colossians 3:5–10:

> Put to death therefore what is earthly in you: sexual
> immorality, impurity, passion, evil desire, and covetous-
> ness, which is idolatry. On account of these the wrath of
> God is coming. In these you too once walked, when you
> were living in them. But now you must put them all away:
> anger, wrath, malice, slander, and obscene talk from your
> mouth. Do not lie to one another, seeing that you have put
> off the old self with its practices and have put on the new
> self, which is being renewed in knowledge after the image
> of its creator.

When Paul lists the earthly issues to put to death, the first one is sexual immorality. I don't point that out to elevate it over other sins, but because we have been dealing with the sexual ethics of the laws of Deuteronomy 22 (the tutor pointing out our sins in preparation for Christ), the use of sexual ethics by an apostle reflecting on what Jesus's forgiveness means for us in the New Covenant of God's kingdom stands out to me as I read it on the other side of Christ's death and resurrection. Note too that at the end of the passage, Paul connects sexual ethics and other moral issues to bearing God's image into the world.

Instructions apparently continue to matter. God still wants us to value what He values and act like Him as His vicegerents in the world. A Jesus-centered understanding of Scripture lifts some constraints of Scripture (the Law in particular), but one could argue that many constraints remain (the essence of the Law summed up in the Greatest Commandment, the proverbs, and New Testament prescriptive passages). But I don't think the concept of constraints is the most fitting for Scripture's commands and instructions. I prefer a different paradigm altogether, one of master builder and instruction manual for his creation. If I think of the master builder's instructions as constraints, I could argue against the limitation of having to put this bolt there to make the steering wheel work. It may feel limiting that the steering wheel should affect the rudder as it does. But in reality, if the master builder designed a boat that way, then that bolt should go there, and that steering wheel does affect the rudder that way. Rail against it all you want, but in the end, if the master builder hands you instructions for the use of the thing he designed and built, you are wise to believe in the value of those instructions.

In that paradigm, arguments I make against the instructions of the Creator sound as if I think I know more about His creation than He does—that I see myself as a wiser engineer than He. I am reminded of another in Scripture who thought he knew better than God, and I am sobered to think of who I most image when I elevate myself above the Creator in thinking I know better than He how His creation best works (see Isaiah 14:12–15).

GOD'S COMMANDS, GOD'S IMAGE

God says in the Bible's instructions that this kingdom, formed by this Creator, works this way. In terms of sexual ethics, God is a god of faithfulness. He never breaks His vows, and He never forgets His steadfast love for His children. Nothing can separate us from that love. He created us to bear His image into the world, and that includes being faithful to our vows, as He is faithful to His. This is how we best function as His creatures in His creation.

We saw earlier that Jesus fulfilled the Old Testament Law, including Deuteronomy 22, so that we are no longer bound by it. Yet the New Testament confirms that we should continue to value and pursue sexual faithfulness and fidelity in our relationships as image bearers of God. Although, in Christ, we are no longer condemned by our failures, we are still called to value such morality for what it brings to human flourishing.

But again we come back to the question, What morality? Specifically what instructions should we continue to keep today? Do we get to cherry-pick the parts of the Bible with which we are comfortable? Or does the Bible itself teach us how to read it and what parts of its instructions should constrain believers today? I have proposed in this chapter that the Bible gives us great insight into which passages apply today and hope that you have seen the value in staying engaged with Scripture, even with the Law, for what it reveals of the character of our Creator and how it instructs us in living in His image. Rather than being scary, such engagement leads to true flourishing.

On my journey out of a fundamentalism that made me skittish around laws, rules, and commandments from Scripture, I eventually became open again to Scripture that explained the character of God in terms of laws and instructions. I began to find parts of the Old Testament Law and wisdom from Proverbs intriguing and actually life-giving. What do God's moral laws teach of Himself? What are we called to imitate from them?

We don't imitate God by either suffering or enforcing the penalty of the Law, for that is something He alone is equipped to judge, and Christ has paid our debt in full. But we can imitate the aspects of His character He shows us through His deep commitment to fidelity in relationships. His faithfulness is the essence of Christianity. That He calls us to such faithfulness with others feels exactly right in light of who He is and what He created us to be. These things can be understood and valued when we accurately handle the Bible, valuing Old Testament commands that have been fulfilled in Christ without projecting them onto others in ways that deny Him, and wisely applying and obeying New Testament commands using Scripture as the guide on how God intended for us to implement them. In the next chapter we will look specifically at several New Testament instructions to women in this light.

Are Paul's and Peter's Instructions Good for Women?

As we approach some particularly hard prescriptive passages in the New Testament written by Peter and Paul, we will use our number one interpretive tool—the Bible is the best commentary on itself—again and again. Does the Bible give similar or different instructions elsewhere? Does the Bible affirm those obeying such instructions throughout Scripture? Does the Bible affirm someone who seems to be doing something different from such instructions? The Bible is a connected, coherent book, and we can use the various ways it addresses a particular issue or instruction to understand that instruction's role in our lives today. As we discussed in the previous chapter, these are New Testament prescriptive passages that still constrain us today. But what exactly do they instruct us to do? God does not leave us as orphans to figure this out. He has left us with His Spirit and the rest of the Bible to aid our understanding.

Note that we will not resolve all questions in the New Testament pertaining to women. I can't imagine that is possible this side of heaven! Even questions that I am able to answer for myself I may not answer for you. I am convinced that the Holy Spirit is able to correctly apply Scripture in the hearts of individual believers. I will hand out thoughts and suggestions in this chapter, and I will share my personal convictions. But in the end, I will leave you to wrestle with the Spirit in your own study of the Word to draw your personal conclusions and private applications. After all, you will never believe with confidence just because I suggest something. But when the Spirit convicts a person through the Bible, those beliefs endure. In that light, I trust Him with all of our hearts as we work with Him to understand Scripture.

THEMES IN THE NEW TESTAMENT

Instructions in the New Testament, even controversial ones, still center on two themes that we saw in the Old. First, be like God. In the Old Testament, we saw that the foundation of our created identity was to image God into His creation. In the New Testament, we are repeatedly reminded that in Christ we are once more equipped to do this. This is especially highlighted concerning instructions to women in Ephesians and 1 Peter.

Theme #1: Be Like God

Consider Peter's instructions to women in 1 Peter 3 and Paul's in Ephesians 5. Paul uses the phrase "Be imitators of God" (Ephesians 5:1) to set up the chapter that includes instructions to wives. Peter says that Christ has left us an example that we should follow in His steps (see 1 Peter 2:21) as the opening salvo in his applications to various groups in the church, including wives of husbands who are disobeying God. We don't need a doctorate in biblical studies to see this theme! Men and women emerged on the scene of creation in Genesis 1 and 2 as image bearers of God. Imaging God is the entire point of the first woman being called a helper to the man. God has called both men and women to reflect His image, and I find it especially helpful that Scripture specifically refers to such image bearing in passages that feel difficult for twenty-first-century women. I find inspiration and motivation in hard words when they are founded on my reflecting something beautiful about my God and my Savior.

Theme #2: Love God and Others

The second theme is the Greatest Commandment. All other instructions hang on the foundation of loving God first and imaging that love to our neighbor. This command is communal, asking us to turn toward God first and then others in love. For instance, in instructions to both husbands and wives in the New Testament, spouses and children are the first line of application for such love, and the community of Christ the next. Whatever husbands and wives will image of God, it must first go through their family and community, not around it.

AVOIDING THE SECRET DECODER RING

As we engage with hard or confusing instructions in the New Testament, I try to avoid what a friend of mine calls the secret-decoder-ring approach. That's when someone refers to an obscure cultural issue not mentioned in Scripture to interpret a passage of the Bible. Of course, these Bible passages were written in and to a particular culture. For instance, we understand the instructions in Romans 14 about curbing our rights for the good of weaker brothers through the cultural issue of eating meat sacrificed to an idol. Grocery store items today are no longer sold after being used in pagan rituals, and the cultural context of Paul's day helps me interpret Romans 14 and apply it for myself today.

Note that Scripture itself informs us of this cultural issue. Both 1 Corinthians 10 and Acts 15 discuss meat offered to idols. Although Acts 15 mentions it briefly, 1 Corinthians 10 offers a long explanation of the issue that Romans 14 speaks of. To fully comprehend these passages, it's valuable to read outside commentary by secular historians, but Scripture itself gives us the needed historical context to understand Paul's point.

Furthermore, the various Bible passages on the cultural issue of meat offered to idols give seemingly opposing instructions. In Acts 15, elders tell early Gentile believers to abstain from meat offered to idols, while in Romans 14, Paul opens the door for each believer to do what his conscience dictates. While these passages center on a particular cultural issue of the day, Scripture still explains the issue to us. It both teaches us the issue and shows us how the application depends on context. The Bible itself gives us the tools of interpretation we need to understand how to approach similar situations today.

In contrast, many use external cultural commentary to explain why a passage in Scripture does not mean what it says. I note this particularly among some commentators speaking of Paul's writings on women in the church and home (see Ephesians and 1 Timothy). Is it possible when we read those passages that we don't know everything the readers of Paul's day knew? Absolutely. But if we take the next step to say that we, then, cannot understand or apply it correctly today, we are entering dangerous territory in interpreting Scripture, battles fought long ago by church fathers to make Scripture accessible to the common man.

THE REAL DECODER RING

Consider for a moment those old fights. For many years, the primary Bible available was written in Latin. Because the common people could not speak or read Latin, the Bible was basically unavailable to them. They relied on church leaders to tell them what the Bible said, and those leaders became known for their corruption and spiritual abuse of believers during that time. Such men as John Wycliffe, Martin Luther, and William Tyndale took the great risk of standing against church authorities of that day to translate the Bible into the language of the common man. Once the Bible became more accessible, the Great Reformation took place.

Those men fought first for a Bible the average man and woman could read, and second for that Bible to be the final authority for church doctrine and practice. As I read through church history and watch modern church practices, I have a strong conviction that these two ideas must continue to constrain the modern church. The Bible is sufficient for faith and practice, we say.

To be clear, I have many books that I refer to when studying the Bible. I am not opposed to outside study helps. This book is one such help. But the best resources rely on the Bible to explain the Bible. Although outside cultural history and commentary are useful, they must submit to what Scripture actually says. Great abuse happens in churches when we are not constrained by the Bible's own words. We should guard ourselves against teaching questionable passages so that they seem understood by only a select few with access to historical documents that the average reader does not have. The real decoder ring for interpreting Scripture is Scripture itself applied by the Holy Spirit. The Bible is not a math book that requires formulas it refuses to provide.

Six Difficult Passages

With that foundation in mind, let's look at several questionable teachings from four New Testament passages referencing women or wives: 1 Timothy 2, 1 Corinthians 11 and 14, and 1 Peter 3. Instead of dealing with every problematic passage that appears in Scripture, I want to examine issues raised in these major ones. You can extrapolate from the principles used here to help you as you wrestle with other issues. I want to both confront questionable passages here and model a method you can use for your own personal study and reflection.

1. Women Teaching with Authority

First Timothy says, "A woman must quietly receive instruction with entire submissiveness. But I do not allow a woman to teach or exercise authority over a man, but to remain quiet. For it was

Adam who was first created, and then Eve" (2:11–13, NASB). We can approach this passage several ways. One way does not view the Bible as a connected whole. According to this perspective, Paul's instruction contradicted previous passages in Scripture, and his instructions then were relative to only the particular culture in which he was teaching. Or one might teach that this passage is absolute because it is among the final instructions of Scripture, and the examples throughout Scripture of women doing more than what Paul seems to suggest here are tossed out as obsolete. Without using the Bible as commentary on itself, we end up either writing off this passage as irrelevant or interpreting it so strictly that women are forbidden to use their spiritual gifts in the church in any way.

But we are approaching Scripture as a unified text in which each progression in God's story reflects both the past and the future. According to this view, Paul was reinforcing something long believed and taught from Scripture (he refers to Genesis before the Fall) that is still relevant today, so we can use the rest of Scripture to reflect on this verse. When I survey Scripture for women affirmed by God, I note a variety of situations that give helpful commentary on what Paul does and does not mean in 1 Timothy 2.

Deborah was one of the judges of Israel: "Deborah, a prophetess, the wife of Lappidoth, was judging Israel at that time. . . . The sons of Israel came up to her for judgment" (Judges 4:4–5, NASB). Judges exercised martial and military leadership in Israel before the kings. Deborah is also called a "prophetess," though her role as judge was different from that of the prophets who spoke the words of God, according to Deuteronomy 18:18.

Junias is mentioned by Paul in Romans 16:7: "Greet Andronicus and Junias, my kinsmen and my fellow prisoners, who are outstanding among the apostles, who also were in Christ before me" (NASB). The Greek wording here translated "outstanding among the apostles" could mean that Junias was well known as an apostle *or* by the apostles, though the use of the Greek for *among* elsewhere suggests she was a part of the apostles, not outside of them.[1] She was well regarded among them either way.

Priscilla discipled men in cohort with her husband: "[Apollos] began to speak out boldly in the synagogue. But when Priscilla and Aquila heard him, they took him aside and explained to him the way of God more accurately" (Acts 18:26, NASB).

Phoebe was a deacon, according to Romans 16:1: "I commend to you our sister Phoebe, a servant of the church" (NIV). The Greek word for "servant" is also translated "deacon" in 1 Timothy 3.[2]

I keep these particular women in mind when reflecting on 1 Timothy 2 because Scripture affirms each of them. Even Paul himself, who wrote the verses in question in 1 Timothy 2, specifically affirmed Phoebe and Junias.

The Greek word for "teach" used in 1 Timothy 2:12 appears many times in the New Testament, and each time it has the straightforward meaning of "instruct."[3] But the Greek word for "exercise authority" is used in only this one instance in the New Testament.[4] Other passages help us determine what this authority refers to. First Timothy 2 doesn't mean that women were not to speak in church at all since other scriptures make it clear that women spoke in church settings at times without rebuke (see Acts

18:26; 21:9; 1 Corinthians 11:5). This verse also doesn't say that women should never informally teach or disciple men, because Priscilla clearly did that. It doesn't mean that a woman is never to be a civil authority, for then Deborah would have been in violation of this passage. First Timothy 2:12 does mean something, though. If I write it off entirely, I stand to lose a lot more in Scripture than I gain from my view of women's rights.

In Paul's words "I do not allow a woman to teach or exercise authority over a man" (1 Timothy 2:12, NASB), the Greek word for "or" can also be translated "not even" or "even." If you read through the verses in which Paul uses the same connecting word in 1 Corinthians, you will see that it links a phrase that clarifies or intensifies the previous phrase nine of the ten times (2:6; 3:2; 4:3; 5:1; 11:14, 16; 14:21; 15:13, 16). You could say it acts like a funnel. It is similar to saying that since fifty is not enough, neither is forty, thirty, or another lesser number.[5] In the case of 1 Timothy 2, since women are limited from teaching, they are also limited from exercising the spiritual authority spoken of in 1 Timothy 3. The context of this passage matters. It is written in the middle of instructions on appropriate corporate worship and feeds right into the qualifications of elders or overseers in the church. Given the examples of women affirmed in Scripture who were discipling or speaking, it makes sense that the teaching Paul discusses in 1 Timothy 2 is clarified by the phrase *exercise authority*. This passage is written in the context of New Testament church authority structures, and the instructions in 1 Timothy 2 bleed neatly into those pertaining to elders and deacons in 1 Timothy 3. Since teaching in worship is limited for women, according to Paul, exercising the authority of an elder must be as well, since teaching is a part of that role in the church. Because teaching with such authority is not inherent in the office of deacon, it makes sense why Paul does not limit women from serving as deacons and affirms Phoebe in that role in Romans 16. Note the progression of thought in the verses when the two chapters are put together:

> I do not allow a *woman* to teach or exercise authority over a man, but to remain quiet. For it was Adam who was first created, and then Eve. And it was not Adam who was deceived, but the woman being deceived, fell into transgression. But women will be preserved through the bearing of children if they continue in faith and love and sanctity with self-restraint. It is a trustworthy statement: if any *man* aspires to the office of overseer, it is a fine work he desires to do. (1 Timothy 2:12–3:1, NASB)*

Without examining other Scripture, I might think that Paul meant that no woman could ever disciple a man. But I see that Priscilla explained the way of God to Apollos. I might think Paul meant that a woman could never talk in a church setting. But according to 1 Corinthians 11:5, he allowed women to both pray and prophesy in the church. When we read Scripture together as a coherent, connected story with one part reflecting on another, a fairly consistent image of God's good plan for women in the church

---

* *Overseer* and *elder* are interchangeable terms in the New Testament. The chapter divisions were not added to the Bible until the Middle Ages. In this case, I think it was unhelpful and unnecessarily divided Paul's thought.

emerges. This passage is in the context of corporate worship and the qualifications of church elders. God created two genders, distinct but overlapping, to reflect His image in the world. There are distinctions in the church, particularly relating to the spiritually authoritative role of elder, or overseer, which Paul reserved for men.

Is this passage good for women? We are called again to consider our definition of *good* here, for many would not see goodness in limiting women from the office of elder in a church or from teaching with spiritual authority in corporate worship. But if we value the distinctions of gender as part of image bearing as much as we do the overlap, we are equipped to consider that maybe God has something good to communicate to us even through such a limitation. The way we see the Bible affirm other women enables us to recognize inappropriate limitations on women in the church. Congregations should wholeheartedly use women in every way that Scripture allows, not out of begrudging duty but because the church needs women this way to bear God's image into the world.

2. Women Speaking in Church

Once we understand 1 Timothy 2–3 this way, we have the tools we need for unlocking 1 Corinthians 14, the other passage that speaks of women keeping silent in churches. Paul writes, "As in all the churches of the saints, the women should keep silent in the churches. For they are not permitted to speak, but should be in submission, as the Law also says. If there is anything they desire to learn, let them ask their husbands at home. For it is shameful for a woman to speak in church" (verses 33–35).

Note the contrast between women speaking and women

being in submission. This indicates that the speaking in question was the opposite of submission, and that fits nicely with the instructions in 1 Timothy 2–3 on teaching with authority. Because Paul just gave instructions for women prophesying and praying in the congregation in 1 Corinthians 11, it fits that this again limits women from speaking in the spiritually authoritative role of elder/overseer—it does not altogether ban women from speaking in a church setting.

Synthesizing Scripture this way protects us from proof texting (using isolated quotes from a passage out of context to establish our own preferred view). Each bit of Scripture we pull together is like a piece of a jigsaw puzzle, somewhat obscured and indecipherable on its own but reflecting a much more accurate picture when put together with the pieces that fit next to it.

When I put these passages together in context, each one reflecting on the other, a vision for women emerges, one in which women are intimately involved in the most important work of the ministry:

- Priscilla discipled Apollos (see Acts 18:26).
- Phoebe carried the book of Romans to the church in Rome (see Romans 16:1–2).
- Euodia and Syntyche partnered with Paul in the gospel (see Philippians 4:2).

This vision also allows for qualified men to work in important ways too, leading and teaching the church as spiritual authorities who reflect Jesus's shepherding of us.

It's important to note that my personal views of church authority structures play into the application here. By conviction, I follow a Presbyterian view of church authority, in which elders are those with spiritual teaching authority, and deacons are those called to serve the needs of the church under the elders' leadership. In this type of authority structure, qualified women can do anything a qualified, non-ordained man can do in the church. In that church structure, I as a woman have been a deacon in a church, which Paul allows in 1 Timothy 3, but because of my personal conviction, I would not serve as an elder. I will not speak here for or against particular church structures, but I understand that the application for you in your denomination or church may be different.

Is this passage good for women? We've seen in this section that the practice of reading Scripture in the context of other verses that talk of similar things is helpful for understanding a passage that has often been used to deny the place of women's giftings in the church.

3. Women Saved Through Childbearing

Paul uses another phrase in 1 Timothy 2 that many find concerning.

> Let a woman learn quietly with all submissiveness. I do
> not permit a woman to teach or to exercise authority
> over a man; rather, she is to remain quiet. For Adam was
> formed first, then Eve; and Adam was not deceived, but
> the woman was deceived and became a transgressor. Yet
> she will *be saved through childbearing*—if they con-
> tinue in faith and love and holiness, with self-control.
> (verses 11–15)

The idea of woman being saved through childbearing is tucked right in the middle of the first passage we worked through. Some have interpreted this to mean that women are saved from hell through a works-related righteousness that includes having babies. But that view denies the most basic tenets of Christianity. We can again use the Bible to explain the Bible, where the same Paul who authored 1 Timothy 2 wrote the words in Ephesians 2:8–9: "For by grace you have been saved through faith. And this is not your own doing; it is the gift of God, not a result of works, so that no one may boast." Either the Bible is a contradictory mess from which no truth can be known, or the apostle Paul meant something different in 1 Timothy 2 from a works-based salvation for women involving pregnancy and childbirth.

There are cultural issues we know from research outside of Scripture that can help us understand what was likely going on in the church at the writing of these words.[6] But the difference in poor uses of culture to understand Scripture is that we will not let the cultural issue undermine the relevance of the Scripture for today. This outside research is helpful, but it must submit to Scripture itself.

The primary god of the audience Paul addressed in 1 Timothy was Artemis of the Ephesians. Legend said that after watching her own mother struggle for nine days with the birth of her twin brother, Apollo, Artemis had special mercy on those giving birth. She was known as a goddess of midwifery in that culture, a culture in which the number one cause of death for women was childbirth.

Paul was teaching Timothy "sound doctrine" in these letters

that challenged the false doctrines in which believers there were steeped (2 Timothy 4:3, NASB). Some believe that one of those false doctrines was that women's lives could be saved through childbirth by appealing to the goddess Artemis. If that was the case, Paul teaches here that faith in Christ, not faith in Artemis, offers us the answer to the consequences of the Fall around childbirth. Perhaps, for a time, this may have even been a literal saving of women's lives as families turned away from Artemis to faith in Jesus Christ. The early church often experienced bold, miraculous events as faith was established in new locations.

Another interpretation for Paul's words is a bit more straightforward: that Paul was reinforcing a consistent truth from Scripture, that despite woman's part in the Fall, she is deeply, integrally valuable to the existence and flourishing of humankind. In 1 Timothy 2:14, he reminds us that it was the woman who was first deceived and became the transgressor. In other religious systems her role in the fall of man would be worth her total annihilation. In Greek mythology in particular, characters who made such a fatal mistake were regularly condemned to eternal torment. Prometheus, for instance, defied Zeus's purposes by returning fire to humanity, after which Zeus condemned him to be chained to a rock as an eagle ate his liver day after day. Atlas has a similar story of epic payback for his role in thwarting the plans of Zeus.

The Bible, in contrast to the religious beliefs of Paul's day, offers immediate hope to the woman despite her role in the Fall. In Genesis 3, the woman's salvation from her fate is declared nearly simultaneously with the Fall she put in motion: "I will put enmity between you and the woman, and between your offspring and her offspring; he shall bruise your head, and you shall bruise his heel" (Genesis 3:15). Before God turns to anyone else after the Fall, He turns toward Satan and basically says, "You will be at war with the woman through her offspring, and her offspring will destroy you." It is through this woman that the fall of man first occurred, but it was also through her that the Savior would come. This is monumental! Instead of annihilation for her role in the spoiling of Eden, God puts the blame on Satan—"Because *you* have done this" (3:14)—and predicts Eve's salvation. She was saved and protected with emphasis on her role in not just the future of humanity but the coming of the Savior himself.

Later in Genesis 3, the Bible refers to Eve as "the mother of all living" (verse 20). If we average out physical size and strength comparisons of women to men, women's norms are consistently smaller and weaker than men's. Yet at even the most brutal points of history, when physical strength and stamina were most valued, women and children were still protected. Why? Because humanity couldn't go on without them. In a world that has oppressed women at every turn in history, in every culture, womankind has been consistently saved from annihilation through her ability to bear children. This is the thing that fundamentally sets a woman's body apart from a man's, and it is powerful.

It is crude to suggest, but men could be completely wiped from the earth, and as long as one jar of semen was preserved, humankind would go on. But not so with women. And in a culture like Paul's that systemically devalued and oppressed women, her ability to have children saved her in some pretty important connotations of the word *saved*. Despite anything projected onto her negatively by the Fall, a woman's very existence was insured because of her unique ability to bear and raise children.

Today this interpretation feels much less relevant. Worldwide life expectancy over the last decade was around seventy years.[7] We also have much better safeguards for the rights of women throughout the world, so cultures don't value women for their ability to have children the way they used to (the primary reason that barrenness in ancient cultures was synonymous with cultural uselessness for a woman).

With this interpretation, Paul is not saying that God singularly values the woman for her ability to bear children. When talking about childbearing as an essential biological function of womankind, it's hard to both treat it as the miraculous thing that it is (a woman's body can incubate the next generation of humanity!) while also respecting that it is not the whole of womanhood. Remember that Ruth was known as a virtuous woman when she was a barren widow. Boaz recognized her valorous contributions to humanity when she was considered unable to have children.

There is one more possible interpretation of Paul's words, and it is the one that seems to me most consistent with the flow of the passage. This interpretation depends not as much on the meaning of the Greek for "childbirth" but from the fact that there is a definite article in the sentence in the Greek, similar to the English word *the*.[8] In 1 Timothy 2:15, the Greek literally reads "through *the* childbearing" or "through *the* childbirth."[9] Historically in the church, many believed that this referred to the birth of *the* Child,

Jesus Christ. In that sense, women and men are saved through the birth of Jesus, who was notably born of a woman rather than appearing miraculously on earth the way angels did from time to time.

Read 1 Timothy 2:14–15 again in that context: "And Adam was not deceived, but the woman was deceived and became a transgressor. Yet she will be saved through [*the Childbirth*]—if they continue in faith and love and holiness, with self-control." Paul's final line about continuing in faith, love, and holiness makes sense with this interpretation, not that the continuance of faith is a work that saves her, but that her perseverance in faith is evidence of the work of salvation that God has done in her. Paul's thoughts parallel Genesis 3, both recounting the woman's place in the Fall while immediately emphasizing her hope in Jesus's coming, noting particularly in both places that He comes through the seed of the woman.

Is this passage good for women? Instead of suggesting that God singularly values a woman for her ability to bear children, I believe in 1 Timothy 2 that Paul is referring back to Genesis 3, when God Himself speaks over the woman her role in the coming rescue of mankind through Jesus Christ. Despite her role in the fall of man and Adam's attempts to blame the entire thing on her, God blamed Satan and then foretold the coming rescue of humankind through the woman, removing her shame and restoring her dignity. This is very good for women!

4. Women Wearing Head Coverings

Consider these words:

I want you to understand that the head of every man is
Christ, the head of a wife is her husband, and the head
of Christ is God. Every man who prays or prophesies
with his head covered dishonors his head, but every
wife who prays or prophesies with her head uncovered
dishonors her head, since it is the same as if her head
were shaven. . . . Judge for yourselves: is it proper for a
wife to pray to God with her head uncovered? Does
not nature itself teach you that if a man wears long hair
it is a disgrace for him? (1 Corinthians 11:3–5, 13–14)

Head coverings have a long history in the church and beyond.
I grew up around conservative groups that required women to
wear head coverings to Sunday worship and knew a good many
women who grew their hair long in deference to this chapter of
the Bible. But after leaving my conservative Bible college, I saw
that few in the Christian circles I frequented seemed affected
by this chapter at all. This passage was like the weird uncle most
everyone avoids at a family reunion. Although mainstream Christians don't debate this passage much (in my experience), most of
us are familiar with the general issue of head coverings in larger
culture, particularly as those from Middle Eastern cultures where
head coverings are expected move to other cultures where they
are not.

Paul lived in a culture in which head coverings communicated something, and he left us a confusing passage of the Bible
in its wake. But in keeping with our view that the Bible is the
best commentary on itself, Scripture gives us data points that are

helpful in understanding this passage. Consider the Nazirite vow that Samson took in obedience to God, described in Numbers 6:2–3, 4:

> When either a man or a woman makes a special vow, the vow of a Nazirite, to separate himself to the LORD, he shall separate himself from wine and strong drink. He shall drink no vinegar made from wine or strong drink and shall not drink any juice of grapes or eat grapes, fresh or dried. . . .
>
> All the days of his vow of separation, no razor shall touch his head. Until the time is completed for which he separates himself to the LORD, he shall be holy. He shall let the locks of hair of his head grow long.

In Numbers 6, a man set apart in God's service was commanded not to cut his hair, whereas in 1 Corinthians 11 Paul says that long hair shames a man. The cultural argument against head coverings (that this meant something in the Corinthian church that does not affect all believers through history the same way) fits, but note that it fits because the Scripture itself, not a historical document outside of the Bible, gives us the example of various hair lengths serving various purposes at various times.

Scripture also gives us another data point that aids us in understanding the issue of a woman's uncovered or shaved head. A woman's shaved head is mentioned in Deuteronomy 21, and these verses are extremely helpful for understanding the context of 1 Corinthians 11.

> When you go out to war against your enemies, and the
> LORD your God gives them into your hand and you take
> them captive, and you see among the captives a beautiful
> woman, and you desire to take her to be your wife, and
> you bring her home to your house, she shall shave her head
> and pare her nails. And she shall take off the clothes in
> which she was captured and shall remain in your house
> and lament her father and her mother a full month. After
> that you may go in to her and be her husband, and she
> shall be your wife. But if you no longer delight in her, you
> shall let her go where she wants. But you shall not sell her
> for money, nor shall you treat her as a slave, since you have
> humiliated her. (verses 10–14)

In this situation, a Jewish man desired a female captive of war. Apart from the law restricting such behavior, this would usually result in sexual coercion and subjugation in their fallen world. Captive women's heads were shaved as a signal of their captivity, a practice throughout the region among Gentiles as well as Jews, but God's children were supposed to treat their captives differently. God's law gave a path to move a woman in this situation from subjugation in captivity to the protected covenant relationship of marriage.

At the end of the instructions in Deuteronomy 21 on how to treat a captive woman, verse 14 uses a word we have seen before, *humiliated*. This is the same word used of Hamor's treatment of Dinah in Genesis 34. It can also be translated "mistreated" or "taken by force."[10] It doesn't necessarily mean sexual coercion, but it can include that. Even with this law that protected a female captive from being turned into a sexual slave, we see that she is still shamed by captivity, treated in a way not reflective of her inherent value as an image bearer of God. It reminds us that the Law at best only restrained sin. And just as the law regarding adultery didn't keep the woman from being thrown at Jesus's feet in John 8, we see that when we fast-forward to Corinth in Paul's day, the laws against the exploitation of captives didn't keep women in Corinth from being used as slaves.

Women in Corinth—likely consisting of Jews, Greeks, and Romans—were still often brought low through sexual subjugation. Modern tourists to Corinth today can hear of the long history of sexual exploitation of captive women around the Acropolis. First Corinthians 11:5 uses the word *dishonors*. Women whose heads were shaved in that culture bore much disgrace. They were humiliated similarly to Dinah in Genesis 34 and the captives referenced in Deuteronomy 21. When we connect these biblical cross-references, a picture emerges of a Corinthian church affected by the subjugation of women in their culture, which included sexual coercion and slavery.

Consider how such slavery has affected marital relationships in particular throughout history. A master owned his female slave, even if she had married another slave (a practice forbidden in many cultures). Families in African American slave communities in the United States were impacted this way. A husband couldn't protect his own wife and children because he didn't have rights of authority over his own marriage and family; the master assumed rights over the bodies of his slave's wife and children. In that sense, Paul in 1 Corinthians 11 was being subversive within slave culture. He elevated the uniqueness of the marital relationship in a culture that often took women as captives and subjected them to slave masters.

In contrast to what I believe Paul was emphasizing in this passage, many approach 1 Corinthians 11 with an inherent suspicion against women based on the misinterpretation of Genesis 3:16 we discussed in chapter 4: "Your desire will be for your husband, and he will rule over you" (NASB).

For those who believe that Genesis 3 teaches that the woman will have a desire to dominate her husband, passages such as 1 Corinthians 11 are simply about husbandly authority. The primary application some people take away from these passages is for women to submit to the men in their lives instead of fighting against their leadership. But if we read the curse in a straightforward way—that the woman has a strong longing for the man but he rules over her oppressively in response—we are not predisposed to interpret 1 Corinthians 11 as being about haughty women trying to put off the limitations of the authority of their husbands. Instead, Paul was advocating for spousal relationships that protected wives from masculine oppression by a slave master who was not committed to her through spiritual covenant. Read the entire passage through that second lens:

> I want you to understand that the head of every man is
> Christ, the head of a wife is her husband [not a slave
> master], and the head of Christ is God. Every man who
> prays or prophesies with his head covered dishonors his

head, but every wife who prays or prophesies with her head uncovered dishonors her head, since it is the same as if her head were shaven [and she was a humiliated slave of another master]. For if a wife will not cover her head, then she should cut her hair short. But since it is disgraceful [or humiliating because it represents slavery] for a wife to cut off her hair or shave her head, let her cover her head. For a man ought not to cover his head, since he is the image and glory of God, but woman is the glory of man. For man was not made from woman, but woman from man. Neither was man created for woman, but woman for man. That is why a wife ought to have a symbol of authority on her head [a symbol of the protected relationship of marriage, not the exploitive relationship of slave], because of the angels. Nevertheless, in the Lord woman is not independent of man nor man of woman; for as woman was made from man, so man is now born of woman. And all things are from God. Judge for yourselves: is it proper for a wife to pray to God with her head uncovered? Does not nature itself teach you that if a man wears long hair it is a disgrace for him, but if a woman has long hair, it is her glory? For her hair is given to her for a covering [to show to others her protected status from exploitation]. (verses 3–15)

The woman's hair in this culture reflected glory and dignity. A shaved head reflected humiliation and subjugation.

Is this passage good for women? Once we get the context of sexual subjugation in a slave culture, we can better understand what Paul was teaching about husbandly authority and why that was good for women in the Corinthian church. This passage that traditionally has either confused people or seemed particularly limiting to women was actually given to protect women from oppression in a fallen culture that often treated them as expendable sexual objects.

5. Women Being Subject to Husbands

We looked at 1 Corinthians 11 from one angle. Now let's consider it from another along with its parallel command in Ephesians 5:

> I want you to understand that the head of every man is Christ, the head of a wife is her husband, and the head of Christ is God. (1 Corinthians 11:3)

> Wives, submit to your own husbands, as to the Lord. For the husband is the head of the wife even as Christ is the head of the church, his body, and is himself its Savior. Now as the church submits to Christ, so also wives should submit in everything to their husbands. (Ephesians 5:22–24)

Some have argued that *head* as used in 1 Corinthians 11 and Ephesians 5 means "source" rather than "authority." The use of *head* as "source" makes sense when you think of the woman being created from the side of the man in Genesis. But it does not make sense when Paul says to the church at Corinth, "The head of Christ is God." Saying that God is the *source* of Christ gets into tricky doctrinal territory about the nature of the Trinity. If Paul was using *head* in its more common meaning of "authority," it fits all three uses of head in this chapter of 1 Corinthians: between God and Christ, Christ and husbands, and husbands and wives.

Luke 22:42 gives us an interaction of submission between the Father and the Son in the Garden of Gethsemane to flesh out what it means that God is the head of Christ: "Father, if you are willing, remove this cup from me. Nevertheless, not my will, but yours, be done." This example of God the Father being the head of God the Son provides a helpful data point for understanding husbands as the head of their wives. Paul linked Christ's unique relationship with the Father with that of husbands and wives. Consider how Christ responded when people tried to convince Him to act apart from the will of His Father. He reminded even His own parents that He was bound to do the will of God the Father, not theirs (see Luke 2:49). Just as Christ has a unique relationship with the Father, a wife has a unique relationship with her husband. No one else is allowed to enter that relationship as an authority and tell her what to do, particularly slave masters in the Corinthian culture.

Many cultures worldwide (including some Christian churches) practice universal male dominance: the idea that woman in general needs to follow man in general. But universal male dominance subverts the unique glory a wife is to her husband. Paul teaches that she is a crown to her husband, and her husband only. He argued that a wife submits *only* to her husband, not some other master, the same way that Christ submitted *only* to the Father. The goal of 1 Corinthians 11:3, then, is to protect the sanctity of the husband-and-wife union from the projection of other male authority over a wife, particularly in the context of female slaves and their masters who used them sexually. Note too that this submission of a wife to her husband does not extend into heaven, as Jesus taught that we are not given in human marriage in heaven (see Matthew 22:30).

· For many, any suggestion of a husband having authority over his wife is problematic. But the problems we see in modern culture that have also infiltrated the church are not primarily from husbands who have learned to love, care, and sacrifice for their wives as Christ's example teaches. There is, however, a massive issue in Christian and non-Christian cultures that calls for women to submit to men everywhere apart from the covenant relationship of marriage. The only thing that makes marital submission work as Paul describes it in 1 Corinthians 11 and Ephesians 5 is that it exists in an established covenant in which there are clear expectations and responsibilities for *both* parties. This is why submission works in the context of church authorities as well. In both contexts, such submission is bound by covenant. In Paul's day (and during the dark history of slavery in the United States), slavery destroyed the bounds of the marriage covenant. It destroyed marriages by introducing another authority into them that did not share the covenant commitment that bound both parties to relationship in the image of God.

While Paul talks in 1 Corinthians 11 about an authority that is unique to the husband and wife relationship, he also talks about mutuality in their relationship. Authority and mutuality are not mutually exclusive ideas, and husbands and wives benefit when they hold them in conjunction. Just four chapters earlier, in 1 Corinthians 7, Paul says that husbands and wives mutually share their bodies. A woman has authority over her husband's body as he has over hers (see verse 4). In 1 Corinthians 11:11–12, Paul says that woman and man in general are interdependent in the Lord: "As woman was made from man, so man is now born of woman." Paul's language reminds us of Eve as the mother of all living.

Coupling 1 Corinthians 7:4 with other New Testament passages about husbands and wives (such as 1 Timothy 5:8), we see that Christian husbands are to care for their wives as Christ cares for the church, a Christian husband who does not care for his wife is worse than an unbeliever, and a wife's submission is unique to her own husband. In 1 Corinthians 11, Paul taught that if a woman's head was uncovered or shaved so that she appeared to be a conquered subject of *another* man or that her husband treated her as a conquered subject, this dishonored the marriage covenant. This called into question the husband's Christian testimony because this was not the way men in Christ were to treat their wives. Instead of bringing glory to him as Proverbs says a wise woman does, she was dressing in a way—without a head covering—that brought shame upon him (see Proverbs 12:4). Her husband was called to treat her with dignity as a co–image bearer of God, not with humiliation as a defeated captive, and her head covering in that culture was a sign of whether or not he was doing so. And remember, in this culture, a woman had no inherent rights other than what her husband, father, or brothers provided for her.

While the husband in 1 Corinthians 11 was to provide his wife protection from sexual exploitation by other men in that culture, there was still the potential for her to be oppressed by her own husband—potential that remains today. When we talk about authority in the church or home, it is important to note that there are limitations on authority in Scripture, including that of husbands and spiritual elders. They are not supreme rulers over all areas for all people, and they too must submit to authority. The Bible gives pretty strong guidelines for the appropriate role of husbands with their wives. Ephesians 5 is the classic passage on this subject, in which husbands are spoken of with a headship that includes laying down their lives in sacrificial service to their wife as Christ laid down His life for the church.

I believe *head* in 1 Corinthians 11 and Ephesians 5 does indicate "authority" rather than "source." But I also see in Scripture clear biblical constraints on such authorities to protect those under them.* In the context of the slave culture of 1 Corinthians 11, the headship of a Christian husband was to be a source of dignity and protection for his wife in a culture in which women were regularly exploited and abused.

Is this passage good for women? When we look at the holistic way God speaks of authority in the church and home and then

---

* I can't emphasize enough that all who hold authority in the body of Christ must also be submitted to their God-given authority as well. We must beware of leaders who want to be authorities in our lives without being submitted in their own.

see Jesus as the ultimate example of what God is calling men in authority toward, a vision of a biblical manhood that blesses the women in their lives begins to emerge. We will flesh this out much more in the next chapter.

6. Wives Living with Disobedient Husbands

We have looked at Paul's controversial words about women in 1 Timothy 2, 1 Corinthians 11 and 14, and Ephesians 5. Peter also presents controversial words to women in 1 Peter 3:1–2: "In the same way, you wives, be submissive to your own husbands so that even if any of them are disobedient to the word, they may be won without a word by the behavior of their wives, as they observe your chaste and respectful behavior" (NASB).

For years, this instruction seemed to me a nice way of telling wives to sit down and shut up. But I recognize now that I had not considered it in context. Note the phrase that opens verse 1: "In the same way." This indicates that Peter was not talking in a vacuum, and his words in these verses were in the context of something else. When I first read this passage in context with 1 Peter 2, a different view of it emerged—one that hearkens back to the first chapters of Genesis on men and women imaging their Creator in the world.

> You have been called for this purpose, since Christ also
> suffered for you, leaving you an example for you to follow
> in His steps, WHO COMMITTED NO SIN, NOR WAS ANY
> DECEIT FOUND IN HIS MOUTH; and while being reviled,
> He did not revile in return; while suffering, He uttered no

threats, but kept entrusting Himself to Him who judges righteously; and He Himself bore our sins in His body on the cross, so that we might die to sin and live to righteousness; for by His wounds you were healed. For you were continually straying like sheep, but now you have returned to the Shepherd and Guardian of your souls.

In the same way, you wives . . . (1 Peter 2:21–3:1, NASB)

This is profound. The context of Peter's instructions to wives is reflecting Christ in their homes!

Consider first the need for these instructions regarding disobedient husbands. We all know that husbands sin—every last one of them. So do wives. And just as women don't always recognize their sin, men often don't recognize theirs. Peter is teaching us, in the context of imaging Christ, a *gospel response* to a sinning husband.

I don't believe that 1 Peter 3 is dealing with behavior that draws a wife into sin. In the context of illegal behavior or behavior involving physical or sexual abuse, the Bible shows different levels of response based on the seriousness of the sin and the breadth of potential victims. Consider Abigail's example in 1 Samuel 25. When her wicked husband provoked King David, she intervened and convinced David not to attack, preventing much bloodshed. Abigail was commended for interceding to limit the scope of the victims of her husband's sin. In contrast, Sapphira's example in Acts 5 shows God's judgment on a woman who followed her husband into sin instead of standing up against it.

When should a wife win over without a word, and when should she step in physically to prevent sin? Sapphira's example shows us the seriousness of submitting to a disobedient husband when it contradicts the clear leading of the Holy Spirit. From Abigail's example, we see the importance of stepping in when the lives and safety of others is at risk. I respect women who have chosen to patiently endure with a hard spouse, hoping for his repentance. But no one should stay in a situation that allows a woman, her children, or others to be harmed. Peter tells wives to influence their husbands toward repentance in quiet, gentle ways. The Bible also tells us to love our neighbor as ourselves (see Matthew 22:39) and advocate for safety and justice for those who can't advocate for themselves (see Psalm 82:1–4). In Abigail, we see a stark situation in which a woman righteously used words and actions to intervene so that many lives were saved, including the one of her disobedient husband, whom God went on to take in death.

If we are not in situations of life and death, safety and destruction, 1 Peter gives wives of disobedient husbands helpful instructions that reflect overarching themes in Scripture: Grace. Patience. Endurance. Hope. Suffering long, like Christ.

Peter tells wives to reflect Christ in their patience with one who is sinning. This certainly fits the overarching narrative of Scripture that starts with woman created as an image bearer of God and then climaxes with Jesus's life, death, and resurrection that equips her once again to live that vision. The instruction Peter gives is not to ignore or minimize sin. It is actually quite the opposite. Consider the story of Sapphira, who looked the other way when her husband sinned against the church by lying to Peter about money from the sale of some land. She fell dead at Peter's feet for her part in aiding in her husband's sin. We know that in 1 Peter 3, Peter cannot be advocating for another wife to do the same thing. The entire premise of the verse is that the wife is aware of her husband's disobedience to the Word and that this disobedience is a problem. Peter's goal in 1 Peter 3 is for the husband to change—for him to be won over—and he is not offering instructions to minimize or ignore sin. In fact, if a husband is in sin, one of the worst things a wife can do to him and those affected is to stick her head in the sand, ignoring or downplaying his sin. A wife might feel as though she is doing her best to just survive, but what she is also doing is enabling. In modern cultural terms, we say she is codependent—so threatened by acknowledging her husband's sin that she denies it and enables him to continue in it.

Instead of telling a wife to ignore or deny a husband's sin, Peter instructs that a calm, nonverbal reaction by a wife to a serious problem in her husband is powerful to move him toward repentance. There is a response to sin that does not rely on words but nevertheless influences others significantly toward repentance and righteousness. But it is only with maturity that most of us will come to believe this. Few grasp that God has methods much more useful for change than the ones we normally use (primarily our words). In terms of a disobedient spouse, not speaking can have more impact than speaking. That is freeing.

Read in context, this instruction to wives takes on new meaning. This isn't "Shut up and stop nagging." The command is to deal with a husband's sin the way Christ dealt with those against Him. He persevered through unjust accusations, closing His mouth to His accusers, but He did it with a long view of God's plan for redemption (see Luke 23:9).

What might this look like practically? If your husband sins against you, Christ's example tells you not to return that sin in kind. Christ entrusted Himself to the One who judges justly (see 1 Peter 2:23). Certainly, acknowledge the sin against you. Again, this is not about minimizing or denying sin. But there is a way to communicate the truth of a spouse's sin that is not manipulative but instead is reflective of the character of Christ: chaste and respectful. It is helpful to communicate when you are not emotional and before the pressure on you causes you to explode. Acknowledge the sin, but don't rely on an abundance of words in doing so.

Second, if your husband sins against someone else, you can still respond with grace: toward your spouse (acknowledging his sin but influencing him toward repentance with respect) and toward those he sinned against (in particular, acknowledging the truth of what he did to them and looking for respectful, nonmanipulative ways to aid in reconciliation between the parties).

Note again that the example Peter gives us is not a woman but Jesus Christ Himself. Peter gives a particular application to wives, but the larger context of these instructions transcends gender and role, for we are all, male and female, called to be conformed to the image of Christ. We are all called to return grace for evil even as we refuse to sweep sin under the carpet. The goal is to rightly deal with sin—to reconcile, to make things right, to help repair the harm done. But it is the kindness of God that draws any of us to repentance, not human words (see Romans 2:4).

Wives, don't underestimate the power of grace-filled, purposeful silence when your husband sins. According to Peter, it is potentially much more persuasive than words. Grace is the most powerful influence toward authentic repentance ever known. But it is not grace if you don't acknowledge the sin in the first place. That is just self-delusion, and it doesn't help anyone.

Is this passage good for women? When we read Peter's words in light of his earlier interaction with Sapphira as well as David's affirmations of Abigail, we see that the long story of Scripture gives wisdom, instruction, and inspiration to women enduring with a disobedient spouse. You are not alone. God is both your example and helper as you navigate such a situation.

When we view these questionable instructions on women via the overarching context of imaging God into the world and then connect the dots to other passages with similar contexts, we get a much clearer picture of God's purposes in these passages. A vision emerges of women bearing God's image into the world as He intended for us at creation. In Christ, there is no condemnation for us when we fail to follow them, yet there is inspiration in them to stay engaged in God's ongoing commission and our role in it—the good works He created us to do as His kingdom comes and He redeems all that was lost in the fall of man.

Are Instructions to Men
Good for Women?

We have discussed the Creation/Fall/Redemption narrative of Scripture in great detail in terms of women. But women do not live their Christian faith in isolation. A Bible that is good for women has to be good for them in its instructions to men as well, particularly if some of those men will be authorities in women's lives. In churches and homes, workplaces and communities, women are in relationship with men working beside them. In the church, men have been influenced and then, in turn, influenced others in ways that were clearly good for women. Yet we also find much evidence in church history of men who have not embraced a biblical ideal of manhood. Some men have used a twisted view of biblical manhood to assume authority they did not have over women. Others have twisted Scripture to lord authority they did legitimately have over others in domineering, harmful ways. Still others have turned their backs on committed covenant relationships altogether, abdicating their authority to the harm of those they were called to serve and protect.

God created men and women to image Him together, serving and protecting His perfect creation. God's Spirit is now re-creating this interdependent image-bearing work of men and women as He redeems His fallen world. How is God re-creating men in His image? What kind of lives are Christian men called toward in the New Covenant (our relationship with God after Jesus's death on the cross)? And is this life to which He calls men, particularly when it involves authority, good for the women around them?

GENDER DIFFERENCES

I presuppose here that there are differences between the two genders. I talked in earlier chapters about a Venn diagram of gender that has great overlap but still allows for distinctions between men and women. We can make two mistakes when approaching a discussion of God-ordained gender differences. First, we can get too scrupulous, going beyond what Scripture actually says. We infer from what the Scripture says, and then we project onto others what we have inferred for ourselves. Although the Spirit will move you or me personally on how to apply gender differences in our own lives, we need not force those distinctions onto others. Scripture is sufficient, and it allows great room in how individuals apply gendered roles personally.

In terms of gender differences, the Bible does not indicate which gender should cook or which should earn more money. It doesn't teach that men do the "important" work while women clean up after them. And it does not extend the dynamics of church and home into the larger culture of government and workplace.

Scripture clearly indicates differences between the two genders, but it doesn't give us the details that many assume or would prefer.

The second mistake—erasing any distinctions at all—is equally harmful. Those who do this often use Galatians 3:28 as their trump card: "There is neither Jew nor Greek, there is neither slave nor free, there is no male and female, for you are all one in Christ Jesus." The problem is that they miss the context of this verse, which is seen in verse 29: "If you are Christ's, then you are Abraham's offspring, heirs according to promise." Jew, Greek, slave, free, man, and woman are all united in the body of Christ. We are all heirs of the promises to Abraham through Christ. We must silence other key scriptures if we believe that Galatians 3:28 erases any distinctions in gender at all. After writing these words in Galatians 3, Paul goes on to speak of gender distinctions in several other places in his letters to the early church. If Scripture is the best commentary on itself, then regardless of what Paul teaches us about the equality of men and women as joint heirs of the promises of God, it does not mean that our Venn diagram of gender is one giant circle of mutually held roles and responsibilities.

When God first uttered the words "Let us make man in our image" in Genesis 1:26 and then created two genders, the plural *our* is noteworthy. God referred to Himself in the plural, and we cannot help but discern something from the fact that He creates two genders to reflect the three persons of Himself. What exactly can we infer? Well, that's a debate over which much ink has been spilled and to which I don't care to contribute anymore. But I will offer some general thoughts for you to ponder and draw your own conclusions. How is the relationship between God the Father, God the

Son, and God the Holy Spirit in the Trinity the model for all human relationship, particularly between the genders? And what does this have to do with a biblical manhood that is good for women?

THREE PERSONS AND TWO GENDERS

The triune God (Father, Son, and Spirit) made mankind (male and female) in His image. Because there are three persons of God and only two genders, there clearly isn't a one-to-one correlation between each member of the Trinity and man or woman. In fact, in the New Testament, both husbands and wives are called to reflect Christ in their marriage, husbands in Ephesians 5 and wives in 1 Peter 2–3. The Trinitarian model—Father, Son, and Holy Spirit as three beings who mysteriously coexist as one—is not about whether women reflect the Spirit more or men reflect the Father more. But we do see in the Trinity a great example of overlap in relationships that still leaves room for distinctions. Jesus said in John 10:30, "I and the Father are one." But in John 14:28, He said, "The Father is greater than I." Jesus called Himself "I am," clearly claiming to be God, and He also spoke of the Father as other than Him, even submitting to the Father during His life on earth in the Garden of Gethsemane.

Similarly, when Jesus spoke of the Holy Spirit in John 14–16, He revealed that the Holy Spirit and Jesus function differently. One could say that the Holy Spirit submits to Jesus's mission rather than one particular to Himself. Consider Jesus's words of the Spirit in John 16:13–14: "When the Spirit of truth comes, he will guide you into all the truth, for he will not speak on his own authority, but whatever he hears he will speak, and he will declare to you the things that are to come. He will glorify me, for he will take what is mine and declare it to you."

What does this model for us in human relationships? We see again the blessed alliance in the Trinity, in which each member values the roles of the others as well as His own. The three work together in harmony, honoring each other, to redeem and restore God's children and to uphold the glory of God's name. In this framework, I see authority and submission in the Trinity, but it is submission in the best sense of the word—an alliance of support of a unified mission equally valued by the Father, Son, and Holy Spirit. In the blessed alliance of man and woman, a biblical manhood that is good for women reflects the blessed alliance of the Trinity.

Consider Ephesians 5, the classic passage on authority and submission in male and female relationships. There the apostle Paul (who also writes in Galatians 3 that male and female are united as recipients of the promises made to Abraham) tells wives to submit to their husbands in marriage and husbands to love their wives as Christ loved the church. As we said in the previous chapter, at face value this passage (which speaks to husbands and wives in particular, not men and women in general) indicates male authority in the home. The other place of authority and submission in male and female relationships is church leadership, particularly the role of elder/pastor/overseer. Though women throughout Scripture were spoken of as prophetesses and perhaps apostles, the specific offices of priest in the Old Testament and elder in the New Testament were limited to men.

Apart from confidence in the beauty of the blessed alliance between genders, those limitations feel scary, especially based on what the Bible, let alone our own personal experience, has shown us of men with unrestrained authority. But just as I don't want my role in the blessed alliance of gender minimized because some women have been adulteresses or manipulators, I don't want to undermine the value of the authoritative role of pastors or husbands because some men have abused their authority.

If the Bible does set up some men in authoritative roles over men and women in their churches and over their own wives in their marriages, it's important that we understand what the Bible teaches about God's vision for such leadership. In earlier chapters, we looked at stories of women such as Ruth, Rahab, and Dinah to help us understand Scripture's larger narrative involving women. Let's look now at a specific man from Scripture on his journey to biblical manhood in the image of Christ, one who arguably had the most authoritative role in the church a human could have.

IMPETUOUS PETER

Examining the life of Peter will aid our understanding of what God calls our brothers in Christ toward in the church and home, particularly when it comes to spiritual authority. After all, Peter was the man on whom Jesus said He would build His church (see Matthew 16:18). The Catholic Church even views Peter as the first pope.* Though Paul wrote more of the epistles, Peter is still a central authoritative figure in the New Testament. We find, however, a great contrast between Peter's authoritative role in the New Testament church after Jesus's ascension and his deportment in the Gospels while walking with Jesus.

Of all the characters described in the Old and New Testaments, Peter is the one with whom I most self-identify. I love Paul, the legalist who finally realized he was the chief of sinners (see 1 Timothy 1:15). I am inspired by Joseph of the Old Testament, who grasped like few others how God's grand eternal plans give perspective to hellish betrayal on earth. I want to meet Ruth, whose steadfastness for someone so new in the faith is striking, and Mary of Bethany, who in John 12 seemed to understand Christ's coming death well before the male disciples as she anointed Him with oil in preparation of His burial. In contrast, it's hard to admire the impetuous, impulsive Peter of the Gospels.

But it's not hard to imagine being like him. At least not for me.

Peter was likely in his early thirties during the years he spent with Jesus in the Gospels. He was married and considered a mature male in his culture, yet he was anything but mature in Christ. When we first meet Peter in the Gospels, he is rash and often blurts out words without thought to their consequences. To which of the disciples did Jesus say, "Get behind me, Satan! You are a hindrance to me" (Matthew 16:23)? That is a harsh word from Jesus!

---

* There is debate on what Jesus meant in Matthew 16:18 when He said to Peter, "On this rock I will build my church." My conviction is that the role of Peter in the church is clarified by how the rest of Scripture speaks of New Testament church leadership. Peter had a major authoritative role, but he submitted to both Christ and other apostles, such as Paul.

In Mark 9, we see Jesus first shaping Peter's understanding of himself and his role in the kingdom of God. Peter and the other disciples argued about which of the disciples would be the greatest (see verse 34). Jesus responded, "If anyone would be first, he must be last of all and servant of all" (verse 35). And in Mark 10:42–45, Jesus taught,

> You know that those who are considered rulers of the Gentiles lord it over them, and their great ones exercise authority over them. But it shall not be so among you. But whoever would be great among you must be your servant, and whoever would be first among you must be slave of all. For even the Son of Man came not to be served but to serve, and to give his life as a ransom for many.

Jesus is clear in this teaching about the humility needed for those leading and holding authority in the body of Christ. You don't seek the first place and the highest honor in the kingdom of God. Instead, you serve, and in so serving, you lead. This hearkens back to the creation mandate of Genesis 1 and 2: to serve and protect. Peter likely nodded along at this point. In the Gospels, he tended to think he understood more than he actually did.

In John 13:3–9, 12–15, Jesus gave Peter a final face-to-face teaching on servant leadership before His death:

> Jesus, knowing that the Father had given all things into his hands, and that he had come from God and was going back

to God, rose from supper. He laid aside his outer garments, and taking a towel, tied it around his waist. Then he poured water into a basin and began to wash the disciples' feet and to wipe them with the towel that was wrapped around him. He came to Simon Peter, who said to him, "Lord, do you wash my feet?" Jesus answered him, "What I am doing you do not understand now, but afterward you will understand." Peter said to him, "You shall never wash my feet." Jesus answered him, "If I do not wash you, you have no share with me." Simon Peter said to him, "Lord, not my feet only but also my hands and my head!" . . .

When he had washed their feet and put on his outer garments and resumed his place, he said to them, "Do you understand what I have done to you? You call me Teacher and Lord, and you are right, for so I am. If I then, your Lord and Teacher, have washed your feet, you also ought to wash one another's feet. For I have given you an example, that you also should do just as I have done to you."

Jesus challenged Peter to let go of his notions of what was appropriate. He called Peter to step out of his comfort zone. Then having demonstrated servant leadership for Peter, Jesus called him to model the same as he taught and led in the future. Jesus focused particularly on Peter when teaching on servant leadership in the Gospels. This makes sense when we consider the crucial role Peter would play by God's own design in the building of the New Testament church. Jesus would place on him the greatest responsibility among the twelve disciples, and the one with the greatest authority must too exhibit the greatest humility. Jesus emphasized this to Peter multiple times.

MORE HUMILITY NEEDED

Yet after Jesus's resurrection in Acts 2, we see that Peter was still a status-conscious Jew concerned about keeping traditional Jewish dietary restrictions. It took a supernatural vision delivered three times to prepare Peter's heart to serve the Gentile Cornelius, whom God was sending to Peter. He began his descent into humility by increasingly defiling himself in terms of the Old Testament ceremonial law that he had previously worked hard to uphold. "He stays with a ceremonially unclean tanner; he is to eat unclean food; he is to go to unclean Gentiles; he is to enter the unclean house of a Gentile."[1] God had to deliberately humble Peter, whom He directed audibly in visions by the Holy Spirit, in order that Peter would take the good news of Jesus to the Gentiles, breaking down the barriers of race, ethnicity, and gender.

But if you follow the story past the book of Acts, we see from Galatians 2, written about Peter around a decade after the gospel came to the Gentiles, that whatever lessons Peter had learned in the Gospels and his interactions with Cornelius in Acts, he had reverted back to protecting his status as a Jew. He was leading in the very pride that Jesus had warned him against in the Gospels, with a hypocrisy that favored status-conscious Jews to the detriment of the Gentile believers.

When Cephas [Peter] came to Antioch, I opposed him to
his face, because he stood condemned. For before certain
men came from James, he was eating with the Gentiles;
but when they came he drew back and separated himself,
fearing the circumcision party. And the rest of the Jews
acted hypocritically along with him, so that even Barnabas
was led astray by their hypocrisy. (verses 11–13)

Paul opposed Peter to his face, but it is important to note that
Peter apparently received the rebuke. Perhaps of all the things we
can learn from Peter, his greatest example of biblical manhood—the essence of the humility God developed in him—is
his response to correction.

PETER DENIES CHRIST

Before Peter listened to Paul's rebuke in Galatians, he received another one from Jesus Himself. Matthew 26 recounts a soul-
wrenching interaction between Jesus and Peter. On the night of
Jesus's betrayal, He told the disciples of the coming crucifixion and
their scattering. Peter rashly proclaimed, "Though they all fall away
because of you, I will never fall away" (verse 33). Yet, just hours
later, Peter denied Jesus—not once, not twice, but three times—
even cursing and swearing that he never knew Him. Luke 22:61
says that Jesus, hanging on the cross, caught Peter's eye in that moment. They exchanged no words, but Peter quickly came to himself, went away, and wept bitterly. Peter had failed Christ miserably

in His darkest hour. His failure was all the more bitter in light of his bold, naive protestations that he would never do such a thing. Peter's pride had tumbled him into a deep, dark place.

John 21 records the first time Peter saw Jesus after the Resurrection. It is beautiful in contrast to the last time Jesus and Peter looked at one another. If anyone should have been ashamed, hiding from Jesus, it was Peter. He failed Christ at His darkest hour. Yet both Peter and Jesus have unexpected reactions. Christ offered no condemnation, and Peter exhibited no shame: "That disciple whom Jesus loved therefore said to Peter, 'It is the Lord!' When Simon Peter heard that it was the Lord, he put on his outer garment, for he was stripped for work, and threw himself into the sea. The other disciples came in the boat, dragging the net full of fish, for they were not far from the land, but about a hundred yards off" (verses 7–8).

While the other disciples made a respectful return in the boat, Peter jumped right into the water and swam/ran to Jesus. He had no pride and put on no earthly pretense. I can imagine the moment for him. They had crucified his Lord, he had denied Jesus, and there was the Savior, standing on the shore. Peter's response reflected his utter need for Jesus: "Jesus, I can't do this on my own. I just denied You three times. I don't know what I'm supposed to be doing now. I can't even catch fish on my own. I'm sitting here fishing on this boat because I have no idea what else I'm supposed to be doing. I need You!" In that moment, nothing else mattered. His shame, the ugly cousin of pride, was preempted by his need of Jesus. Getting to Jesus was his number one priority.

After that scene, Jesus gave Peter a chance to affirm his love the same number of times Peter had denied Him. And each time,

Jesus tasked him with the great responsibility: "Feed my sheep" (see verses 15–17). Do you see the great mercy and grace Christ deliberately showed Peter and deliberately recorded for us in His Word? Peter got it wrong more times than he got it right in the Gospels, yet Jesus told him that God would build His house upon Peter the Rock!

GROWING IN HUMILITY

Peter still had much learning to do after Jesus's ascension, but he remained willing to learn. It took decades, but he responded to God's discipline. He learned from Cornelius and received Paul's rebuke. A final snapshot from the life of Peter comes in 1 Peter 5. At this point, Peter was in his early sixties. Listen to Peter's words to the elders of the church, especially in light of the starting point in his journey as a leader wanting to lord authority over others:

> I exhort the elders among you, as a fellow elder and a witness of the sufferings of Christ, as well as a partaker in the glory that is going to be revealed: shepherd the flock of God that is among you, exercising oversight, not under compulsion, but willingly, as God would have you; not for shameful gain, but eagerly; not domineering over those in your charge, but being examples to the flock. And when the chief Shepherd appears, you will receive the unfading crown of glory. Likewise, you who are younger, be subject to the elders. Clothe yourselves, all of you, with humility toward one another, for "God opposes the proud but gives grace to the humble."

> Humble yourselves, therefore, under the mighty hand of
> God so that at the proper time he may exalt you, casting all
> your anxieties on him, because he cares for you. (verses 1–7)

I tear up when I read this passage knowing Peter's own journey. After decades of stops and starts, learning and forgetting,
Peter demonstrated an understanding of what Jesus taught him
years before. He had internalized Jesus's teaching on servant leaders from the Gospels and was now passing it along to others. It
took years of being humbled himself, but finally he was the leader
Jesus taught him to be and modeled for him—a leader God
greatly used to build His church.

Peter emerges in the book bearing his name as a man who
truly valued servant leadership in the image of Christ, instructing
others against the very domineering, shame-based leadership that
God had pounded out of him over the years. Peter gives us an
idea of what to look for in a leader: not a pretense of perfection but
a willingness for correction. Peter was willing to hear rebuke from
both those leading him and those to whom he was supposed to
minister. He modeled a willingness to turn back toward Jesus in
humble repentance again and again. He then was able to lead
others in ways that blessed them, not oppressed them.

To explain this process, my pastor used the illustration of
copper engravings. Making an engraving starts with a hard metal
mold. A softer copper metal sheet is held against the mold and
pounded into the shape. In this illustration, Jesus's teaching is the
hard metal mold, and in Peter's life, it was combined with life
circumstances over many years as God pressed him into that

mold. In the end, Peter reflected Jesus's humility as a leader in beautiful ways.

The first part of 1 Peter 5:6 is often translated "Humble yourselves." But the Greek wording is actually in passive voice. It is not for us to humble ourselves but for us to allow ourselves to be humbled.[2] Humbling ourselves is futile, and people who try to accomplish humility on their own are usually full of themselves in the end. As Martin Luther humorously said, "True humility does not know that it is humble. If it did, it would be proud from the contemplation of so fine a virtue."[3] We can, however, yield to the mighty hand of God and allow Him to humble us. When we read 1 Peter 5, it is important that we recognize that Peter didn't humble himself; God humbled him.

Peter's instructions to elders in the church are to exercise their oversight—to lead but not with a domineering, secular-leadership mind-set. Peter instructs them to lead as Christ modeled in the Gospels: laying down His life for those under His care, washing their feet, and serving. This, too, is what Paul calls husbands to do with their wives in Ephesians 5. Christ again is the model, the metal form in which the copper plate of a husband is being pounded. "Christ loved the church and gave himself up for her," Paul says in verse 25.

Legend tells us that only a few years after Peter wrote 1 Peter 5 to elders in the church, he was martyred. He died as a servant leader, a witness to the church of Jesus's teaching and example. Peter shows us what goes wrong in Christian leadership as well as how it can go right when a man repents and is conformed to the image of Christ in his leadership roles.

THE VALUE OF HUMBLE MASCULINITY

A biblical manhood, particularly of men in positions of leadership, that is good for the men and women around them reflects humility, restraint, and sacrifice. Fathers should not exasperate their children (see Ephesians 6:4). Husbands should sacrificially love and serve their wives (see Ephesians 5:25). And pastors should humbly shepherd their congregations (see 1 Peter 5:2). What did the Good Shepherd do? He laid His life down for His sheep. Domineering authority in the name of Christ is hypocrisy to be rebuked. But a manhood that loves and serves like Christ bears God's image into the world for the good of us all. I believe that the Bible is good to women through its instructions to men, particularly to men in authority. When Peter finally grasped what Jesus modeled for him, his use of authority blessed those under his leadership. Peter was at his best when he was most like Christ. The manhood the Bible instructs is best seen directly through the God-man Himself, Jesus Christ.

In our churches and our marriages, this is the kind of leadership toward which God is calling men. It is a servant leadership, in which the leader lays his life down for those under his care. When men in the body of Christ, particularly those in leadership, allow themselves to be humbled, molded into the image of Christ through life circumstances as Peter was, a biblical manhood emerges that is good for all of us, male and female. Such humility is the soil in which the blessed alliance between the genders can grow and flourish.

Is God Good for Women?

We opened this book with the observation of the fork in the road between orthodox Christianity and second-wave feminism in the twentieth century. Gloria Steinem famously said a feminist is "anyone who recognizes the equality and full humanity of women and men." Is God then a feminist by her definition? If feminism in its purest sense is the quest for justice and equal rights for women, then, yes, God was the first feminist. God created woman in His image and bestowed on her equal dignity with man. The US Declaration of Independence uses the phrase "unalienable rights," rights that stem inherently from our very creation. By a woman's mere existence, God has bestowed on her dignity and privileges that transcend race, economic status, and physical ability.

But sin entered the world, and the inherent dignity of men and women has often gotten lost as corrupt people with power oppress others without it. In Christ, whether we hold power in our culture or not, God equips us once again to live as image bearers of Him, living in light of our inherent dignity in Him while treating others in the hope of their own. God's feminist ideals don't correlate one to one with the world's secular ones; in fact, it is nearly impossible to value women and put forth their needs and rights correctly without first valuing the God in whose image they were made. But understand that any rights we should demand for women worldwide arise from the fact that God created them with those rights and that only He can rightly limit them.

WHERE FEMINISM GOES ONE WAY, THE CHURCH THE OTHER

Where are the forks in the road between God's feminist ideals and those of fallen man? Why have Christians rightly fought for a woman's right to vote but continue to protest abortion vehemently? Of course, Christians see commands against murder as critical to the abortion debate. But there is another issue as well.

We must note the differences in a modern Western view of feminism and the justice for women that Scripture models. The fork in the road seems to center on the concept of independence. Western women's rights discussions often focus on the fact that woman is an autonomous self and no one can tell her what to do. In the case of abortion, the Supreme Court gave the woman absolute rights over her body. The desires of the father of her baby and the welfare of the baby must take a lesser place than her desires for herself. Her autonomy from others is the highest ideal, and woe to those who attempt to influence society against such a choice.

The Bible never supports such independence. Scripture first presents a story of humankind utterly dependent on God. Then it lays a foundation of male and female interdependence. From the first moment man and woman entered the scene—well before the fall of man—they were interdependent. "Bone of my bones and flesh of my flesh," Adam marveled at the woman (Genesis 2:23). Their stories continued to be entwined through God's description of the consequences of the Fall. For good and for bad, men's and women's lives have been joined in the body of Christ ever since. Instead of a social justice that gives woman complete independence from man, God wrote a story that advocates social justice in interdependent relationships between men and women. God lifts up women but not in a way that frees woman from dependence on man or man from dependence on woman. The Bible's instructions to men and women work in covenants of mutual responsibility—be it the covenant relationship of Christian marriage, the covenant relationship of the church, or both—not in barriers between them.

Some versions of modern feminism advocate an independence that diminishes the nobility of women laying down their rights to strongly help others. American individualism, in particular, causes many to miss the value of someone like Ruth, for instance. Feminists may appreciate Ruth's strength, but some would despise her vulnerability. Yet Ruth had both. Notably capable and valorous to Boaz, she still sought his covering. Her need for protection didn't diminish her nobility, and her submission to God's plan did not undermine her value. Instead, it was integral to it.

A BETTER FEMINISM

God's feminist ideals of justice and the full humanity of women tweak our weaker Western ones. If we value the God in whose

image woman was made, we will value the woman herself.
Though God doesn't write a story that supports woman's complete independence from man, He does write one with a much
stronger sense of justice for the weak than the traditional American view of justice offers. In America, we refer to blind justice,
and we often see outside courthouses a statue of a woman blind-
folded holding a set of scales. The blindfold represents objectivity.
But a blind statue weighing pros and cons is not the best illustration of God's justice. Instead, God sees. And He calls us to a justice that takes the blindfold off and judges in favor of those
without resources—those who cannot advocate for themselves.
Look at Isaiah 1:17:

> Learn to do good;
> seek justice,
>   correct oppression;
> bring justice to the fatherless,
>   plead the widow's cause.

Instead of a blind statue weighing pros and cons, God's justice
is revealed in those with resources and power actively seeking those
without to plead their case and bring them the justice they de-
serve as image bearers of God. God disproportionately favors those
who cannot earn for themselves. Consider Jesus's words in Luke
6:32–36 on reflecting God to those who can't or won't repay us:

> If you love those who love you, what benefit is that to you?
> For even sinners love those who love them. And if you do

good to those who do good to you, what benefit is that to you? For even sinners do the same. And if you lend to those from whom you expect to receive, what credit is that to you? Even sinners lend to sinners, to get back the same amount. But love your enemies, and do good, and lend, expecting nothing in return, and your reward will be great, and you will be sons of the Most High, for he is kind to the ungrateful and the evil. Be merciful, even as your Father is merciful.

We often note this passage for its command to love our enemies. The entire chapter of Luke 6 gives strong exhortation to overcome evil against us with a gracious response. But this passage also teaches us to do good to those who cannot return it and to lend to those who cannot pay us back. Then we will be children of the Most High. Then we will reflect God's mercy—mercy He showed even before the fall of man when He created in perfection, and bestowed with every blessing, a man and a woman who had no ability to return the favor. We are to be gracious, seeking in particular to bless those who cannot bless us in return because that is how we image our Father in heaven. Such bestowing of favor and dignity on someone who cannot return it is the essence of His character.

This remains God's call to His image bearers. To the poor, to orphans, to widows—to any who cannot provide or advocate for themselves—God's image bearers aim their resources and seek their benefit as God seeks ours. God's people should create level playing fields for women in our world. We should affirm the full image-bearing humanity of all women. But, in the image of God,

His daughters in this paradigm sometimes lay down their rights for the good of another in God's interdependent family. In a modern context, we would both protest Esther's enslavement and honor her for laying down her rights in service to her people. Her nobility is not diminished because she humbly worked within the unjust system forced upon her.

The bottom line of image bearing for believers in Christ on this side of the Cross is found in 1 Peter 2:23. Jesus entrusted Himself to the One who judges justly, and we are called to do the same. In fact, community and interdependent relationships in Christ are virtually impossible without a confidence in One who is bigger than we are, who sees all and always judges correctly. As we conform to Jesus's example, we see that faith and trust are the foundation of it. We cannot endure like Christ in community, male or female, without trusting our Father in heaven.

A Long but Good Story

This leads us back to the beginning of this book, where I encouraged you, if you aren't sure what you believe about the Bible, to be open to considering its goodness. Although we started this book urging that openness, we likely cannot progress any further in answering the question posed in the title without it. In truth, I cannot imagine someone finding the Bible good if that person doesn't believe in a God whose eternal purposes give meaning to its hard stories. How can we find a Bible about men and women imaging God in the world good if we don't believe in a good God who is worth imaging in the first place?

So is the Bible good for women? The Bible that speaks of the humiliation of Dinah and the exultation of Ruth. The Bible that commands the stoning of the adulteress and then tells of Jesus stopping that punishment just before the act. The Bible that speaks of the reality of shamed captives and then instructs women why they should not live like them. This Bible, understood through Jesus and His role in the long story of Scripture, is indeed very good for women.

Throughout history, some have tried to thwart God's way and His instructions, ignoring them altogether or perverting them to apply them in a way God never meant them to be used. In the example of the young girls of western Nepal mentioned in the introduction, any relationship to Old Testament Law is a *perversion* of God's intent. As I said in the introduction, it projects onto girls on their periods shame the Bible never does, it applies to girls something without the parallel application to men, and it continues a practice that Jesus two thousand years ago said was brought to completion through Him. When we understand Scripture this way, we are equipped for deeply good things that both biblical womanhood and manhood accomplish.

I imagine the path of Scripture as a long, winding road through a mountainous landscape that nevertheless takes us toward our destination. Perversions and misuses of its commandments draw people off the path. Instead, God repeats themes throughout it to keep us grounded in its fundamental purposes. When we connect the dots that Scripture gives us, we honor the Author of Scripture and use it as He intended. The Bible again and again gives us data points to connect so we can live as holistic image bearers of God—for the purposes of the title of this book, so that we can live His *good* plan for us.

But we cannot image God without faith in Him. Living in the full humanity for which God created us depends on faith and relationship with Him, and such faith brings value to interdependent relationships between the genders in which each lays down its rights for the other. Step into this journey. In Christ, you do not walk it alone. You walk it out in an alliance, a coalition among like-minded believers for a common goal: the redemption of Eden.

Christians have long identified with J. R. R. Tolkien's elaborate story begun in *The Fellowship of the Ring.* We resonate with the noble and dangerous quest to destroy the ring that caused so much evil and the detailed cooperation, led by Frodo and Aragorn, that accomplished the goal. And we admire Frodo's faithful companions—Merry, Pippin, and Samwise Gamgee—for stubbornly refusing to leave his side.

> You can trust us to stick to you through thick and thin—to the bitter end. And you can trust us to keep any secret of yours—closer than you keep it yourself. But you cannot trust us to let you face trouble alone, and go off without a word. We are your friends, Frodo. Anyway: there it is. . . . We know a good deal about the Ring. We are horribly afraid—but we are coming with you; or following you like hounds.[1]

Tolkien's story begins with a fellowship, a community. That fellowship breaks, but it is restored in the end. Apart, the members achieve bits and pieces of the final goal. Together, their mutual contributions complete a great restoration. In Christ, we are called to such a noble mission. And we are called to it in community, the fellowship of the Cross.

Our Father in heaven values women. He revealed His goodness, care, and noble plans for women through His revelation of Himself to us in the Bible. The Bible is good for women, and it is good for men. It sets us out on an important, eternal journey and calls us to walk it together in community. Like Him.

Discussion Questions

Introduction

1. Have you personally experienced gender-based oppression? If so, did biblical instructions seem to help or make it worse?
2. Can you identify any presuppositions or suspicions you bring to a discussion of gender in the Bible?
3. How do you feel about the disparate nature of gender? Do you feel more comfortable with an emphasis on distinctions or on overlap? Why?
4. The Bible makes audacious claims about itself in such texts as Psalm 119:105, 2 Peter 1:20–21, and 2 Timothy 3:16–17. What do you think of these claims?
5. Do you more identify with God as Engineer and the Bible as data points, or with God as Author and the Bible as story? How do God and the Bible exhibit both?

Chapter 1: How Did Jesus Approach the Bible?

1. Did you learn Bible lessons as a child? As a grown-up? Does the separate-file-folder approach to teaching moral lessons from the Old Testament resonate with you?

2. Which parts of Scripture that are rarely discussed are you interested in understanding better?

3. In what ways do you easily see Jesus in the Old Testament? In what areas is it difficult to see Him?

4. Think of a hard-to-understand passage or story from the Old Testament. Does it fit any of the categories from pages 28–29 for pointing to Jesus?

CHAPTER 2: WHAT WAS GOOD IN THE BEGINNING?

1. What do you think of the concept of God creating you to be His vicegerent in His creation? How have humans done this in general? How have Christians done this specifically?

2. How do God's command to Adam to work and keep the garden and Jesus's command to His disciples to go into all the world teaching of Christ relate to each other? How are they different? What do you see as your role in either or both?

3. Have you heard teaching that marriage is the ultimate goal for man and woman? Do you agree? Why or why not?

4. From this study of Genesis 1 and 2, what do you see as the benefit to God's creation of His making two distinct but overlapping genders?

CHAPTER 3: WHAT WERE WE MADE TO BE?

1. What connotations do you associate with the word *help*? How does God's example of help challenge those?

2. What do the stories of women like Rahab and Esther reveal to you about help in the image of God?

3. Have you been taught Proverbs 31 as a list of hard-and-fast requirements for women? What principles rather than laws from Proverbs 31 does the Holy Spirit convict you to apply?

4. Have you considered Ruth a woman of valor like the Proverbs 31 woman? How does Ruth as a barren widow clarify what it means to be an 'ishshah chayil in God's image?

CHAPTER 4: HOW DID IT ALL GO WRONG?

1. Considering God's perfect creation of Genesis 1 and 2, what relationships in your life particularly need redemption?

2. Have you seen man's idolatry of work and woman's idolatry of man play out generally and specifically in your life and relationships? In what way?

3. What coping mechanisms have you developed for the problems the Fall has caused between genders? What coping mechanisms have others developed in relationship with you?

4. How does the confident access you can have to God through Christ affect the problems in your life brought about by the Fall? Do you make use of this access you have to God?

CHAPTER 5: IS IT GOING TO GET BETTER?

1. How do you react to Jesus's words to the man seeking eternal life (see Mark 10)? Do Jesus's words feel unfair? Why or why not?

2. How do you define *the good life*? How does your view compare with Jesus's in the Gospels?

3. How did communal good feed individual good in Rahab's life?

4. How does communal good feed individual good in God's kingdom in general? How might it in your life?

CHAPTER 6: IS THE LAW GOOD FOR WOMEN?

1. What is your first reaction to Dinah's story? How do you respond to the instructions in Deuteronomy 22 for rape survivors to marry their rapists?

2. How difficult is God's rigid call to sexual faithfulness in Deuteronomy 22? How is it reflective of His character?

3. God commanded Hosea to pursue Gomer, not to stone her according to the Law but to buy her from her slavery and restore her as his wife. What does this tell you about the character of God in the laws of Deuteronomy 22?

4. Have you experienced Christians heaping extra shame on the abused? How do you think Christians should respond to sexual abuse to reflect the image of God?

CHAPTER 7: WHAT INSTRUCTIONS ARE FOR TODAY?

1. Have you had a particular Scripture used against you? Was it prescriptive or descriptive? According to what we have

learned in these chapters, do you believe that the passage describes guidelines required of Christians today, or is it something fulfilled in Christ?

2. What does it mean to you to approach morality in the Bible from a position of grace in Christ?

3. Which Old Testament laws reflect modern ideals of social justice?

CHAPTER 8: ARE PAUL'S AND PETER'S INSTRUCTIONS GOOD FOR WOMEN?

1. Have you been taught secular historical information to better explain a Scripture passage? Do you think it was well handled, or did it contradict Scripture?

2. How do the examples of Deborah, Junias, Priscilla, and Phoebe help you understand Paul's instructions to women in 1 Timothy 2?

3. What do you think Paul meant when he said that woman would "be saved through childbearing" (1 Timothy 2:15)? Does this seem good for women or objectifying?

4. Does linking headship in 1 Corinthians 11 to captivity in Deuteronomy 21 help you understand the passage? Why or why not?

5. Have you experienced a time when your words worsened a situation instead of helping someone see his error? What do you think of Peter's instructions to wives to win over their husbands without words?

CHAPTER 9: ARE INSTRUCTIONS TO MEN GOOD FOR WOMEN?

1. Who in Scripture seems a good example of what God intends a man to be in His image? Who in your life?
2. Does the person you admire in real life exhibit humility like Christ? How?
3. Does the person you admire in real life have authority? If so, how does he lead through service?
4. Does the person you admire in real life repent or own his mistakes?

CHAPTER 10: IS GOD GOOD FOR WOMEN?

1. How is God's feminism similar to secular feminism? How is it different?
2. In your personal life, how has secular feminism helped you? How has it harmed you?
3. How do you envision living out God's image in your community, particularly as a woman?
4. Has there been a time you had to lay down your rights for the good of the community? Did that seem oppressive to you or noble?
5. Do you have a community in Christ? If so, how do you see yourself contributing to its flourishing in the image of God?

Notes

Introduction

1. Jane Greenhalgh and Michaeleen Doucleff, "A Girl Gets Her Period and Is Banished to the Shed: #15Girls," *NPR*, October 17, 2015, www.npr.org/sections/goatsandsoda /2015/10/17/449176709/horrible-things-happen-to-nepali -girls-when-they-menstruate-15girls.

2. *Statistical Yearbook of Nepal—2013* (Kathmandu, Nepal: Central Bureau of Statistics, 2013), 23, http://cbs.gov.np /image/data/Publication/Statistical%20Year%20book%20 2013_SS/Statistical-Year-book-2013_SS.pdf.

3. National Woman's Christian Temperance Union, www .wctu.org/history.html.

4. Phyllis Trible, *Texts of Terror: Literary-Feminist Readings of Biblical Narratives* (Philadelphia: Fortress, 1984).

5. See, for instance, Carolyn McCulley, *Radical Womanhood: Feminine Faith in a Feminist World* (Chicago: Moody, 2008).

6. Saint Augustine, *On Christian Teaching,* trans. J. J. Shaw (Digireads.com Publishing, 2009), 22.

1: How Did Jesus Approach the Bible?

1. Carolyn Custis James, *When Life and Beliefs Collide: How Knowing God Makes a Difference* (Grand Rapids, MI: Zondervan, 2001), 42.

2: What Was Good in the Beginning?

1. James Strong, *The New Strong's Exhaustive Concordance of the Bible* (Nashville: Thomas Nelson, 1990), s.v. "tselem."

2. Dictionary.com, s.v. "vicegerent," www.dictionary.com /browse/vicegerent?s=t.

3. Strong, *Exhaustive Concordance,* s.v. "abad," "shamar."

4. Mary A. Kassian and Nancy Leigh DeMoss, *True Woman 101: Divine Design: An Eight-Week Study on Biblical Womanhood* (Chicago: Moody, 2012), 11.

5. Carolyn Custis James, *Half the Church: Recapturing God's Global Vision for Women* (Grand Rapids, MI: Zondervan, 2011), 137.

3: What Were We Made to Be?

1. Hannah Anderson, *Made for More: An Invitation to Live in God's Image* (Chicago: Moody, 2014), 23.

2. *Bible Study Tools,* s.v. "tselem," www.biblestudytools.com /lexicons/hebrew/nas/tselem.html.

3. *Bible Study Tools,* s.v. "ezer," www.biblestudytools.com /lexicons/hebrew/nas/ezer-2.html.

4. See Joshua 2; Judges 4-5; Ruth 1; Esther 4; Luke 10; Acts 18; Romans 16; Philippians 4.

5. Wendy Alsup, *The Gospel-Centered Woman: Understanding Biblical Womanhood Through the Lens of the Gospel* (North Charleston, SC: CreateSpace, 2012), 85–86.

6. *Bible Study Tools,* s.v. "ishshah," www.biblestudytools.com /lexicons/Hebrew/nas/ishshah-2.html and s.v. "chayil," www .biblestudytools.com/lexicons/hebrew/nas/chayil.html.

4: How Did It All Go Wrong?

1. See Genesis 4–11 for the stories of Cain, Abel, Noah, and the Tower of Babel.

2. *Oxford Dictionaries,* s.v. "redemption," www.oxforddictionaries .com/us/definition/american_english/redemption.

3. C. S. Lewis, *The Silver Chair,* The Chronicles of Narnia #4 (New York: HarperCollins, 1994), 254.

4. *Bible Study Tools,* s.v. "mashal," www.biblestudytools.com /lexicons/hebrew/nas/mashal.html.

5. Adam Taylor, "The Facts—and a Few Myths—about Saudi Arabia and Human Rights," *Washington Post,* February 9, 2015, www.washingtonpost.com/news/worldviews/wp /2015/02/09/the-facts-and-a-few-myths-about-saudi-arabia -and-human-rights.

6. Sarah O'Meara, "The Problem of Too Many Baby Boys in China," *Aljazeera,* March 14, 2015, www.aljazeera.com /indepth/features/2015/03/problem-baby-boys-china -150305051058735.html.

7. The documentary *It's a Girl* (www.itsagirlmovie.com) explores the systematic devaluing of female infant lives in various cultures worldwide.

8. Susan T. Foh, "What Is the Woman's Desire?" *Westminster Theological Journal* 37, no. 3 (Spring 1975): 383, www .galaxie.com/article/wtj37-3-04.

9. James Strong, *The New Strong's Exhaustive Concordance of the Bible* (Nashville: Thomas Nelson, 1990), s.v. "tshuwqah."

10. Saint Augustine, *St. Augustine Confessions,* book 1, chap. 1, www.ourladyswarriors.org/saints/augcon1.htm#chap1.

11. I expound on this more in my self-published work *The Gospel-Centered Woman: Understanding Biblical Womanhood Through the Lens of the Gospel* (North Charleston, SC: CreateSpace, 2012).

5: Is It Going to Get Better?

1. Dictionary.com, s.v. "self-actualization," www.dictionary.com/browse/self-actualization.
2. Corrie ten Boom, *The Hiding Place* (Ada, MI: Baker, 2006), 229.
3. Ram Goli, "Amazing God in the Maze of Dating," *Boundless,* April 10, 2015, www.boundless.org/blog/amazing-god-in-the-maze-of-dating.

6: Is the Law Good for Women?

1. Rachel Held Evans, *A Year of Biblical Womanhood: How a Liberated Woman Found Herself Sitting on Her Roof, Covering Her Head, and Calling Her Husband "Master"* (Nashville: Thomas Nelson, 2012), 66.
2. Matthew Kaemingk, "Pacific Northwest Religion: Doing It Different, Doing It Alone Part I," *Christ & Cascadia,* October 25, 2013, www.christandcascadia.com/religion-in-the-pacific-northwest-doing-it-different.
3. Rod Nordland, "Rape Victim Faces Honour Killing," *The Hindu,* July 21, 2014, www.thehindu.com/news/international/world/rape-victim-faces-hounour-killing/article6231194.ece.

4. Zack Eswine, *Sensing Jesus: Life and Ministry as a Human Being* (Wheaton, IL: Crossway, 2012), 167.

7: What Instructions Are for Today?

1. *Merriam-Webster,* s.v. "prescriptive," www.merriam-webster .com/dictionary/prescriptive.
2. *The Free Dictionary,* s.v. "descriptive," www.thefreedictionary .com/descriptive.
3. Some commentators believe that the sacrifice of the daughter of Jephthah was that she was to remain a virgin throughout her life rather than that she was killed as a human sacrifice.

8: Are Paul's and Peter's Instructions Good for Women?

1. *Bible Hub,* http://biblehub.com/greek/1722.htm.
2. *Bible Study Tools,* s.v. "diakonos," www.biblestudytools.com /lexicons/greek/nas/diakonos.html.
3. *Bible Study Tools,* s.v. "didasko," www.biblestudytools.com /lexicons/greek/nas/didasko.html.
4. *Bible Study Tools,* s.v. "authenteo," www.biblestudytools .com/lexicons/greek/nas/authenteo.html.
5. *Bible Hub,* s.v. "oude," http://biblehub.com/greek/3761 .htm.
6. Sandra L. Glahn, "The First-Century Ephesian Artemis: Ramifications of Her Identity," *Bibliotheca Sacra* 172 (October–December 2015): 50–69.

7. "Life Expectancy," *World Health Organization* (blog), www.who.int/gho/mortality_burden_disease/life_tables /situation_trends/en.

8. William Mounce, *Word Biblical Commentary: Pastoral Epistles, Vol. 46* (Nashville, TN: Thomas Nelson, 2000), 145.

9. *Bible Hub*, s.v. "teknogonia," http://biblehub.com/greek /5042.htm.

10. *Bible Study Tools*, s.v. "anah," www.biblestudytools.com /lexicons/hebrew/nas/anah-4.html.

9: Are Instructions to Men Good for Women?

1. Hans F. Bayer, *Apostolic Bedrock: Christology, Identity, and Character Formation According to Peter's Canonical Testimony* (Crownhill, UK: Paternoster, 2017), 280.

2. *Bible Hub*, s.v. "tapeinoó," http://biblehub.com/greek/5013 .htm.

3. Martin Luther, *Martin Luther Christmas Book* (Minneapolis: Augsburg, 1948), 164.

10: Is God Good for Women?

1. J. R. R. Tolkien, *The Fellowship of the Ring: Being the First Part of the Lord of the Rings* (New York: Del Ray, 2012), 118.

Canto is an imprint offering a range of
titles, classic and more recent, across a
broad spectrum of subject areas and
interests. History, literature, biography,
archaeology, politics, religion, psychology,
philosophy and science are all represented
in Canto's specially selected list of titles,
which now offers some of the best and
most accessible of Cambridge publishing to
a wider readership.